Organizational Design *that Sticks*!

Organizational Design *that Sticks!*

Dr. Dale J. Albrecht

Alonos®
© 2018

First Printing: 2018

ISBN-13: 978-1-948699-00-6

Alonos®
Dallas, Texas, United States of America

www.Alonos.com

Alonos® is a registered trademark of the Alonos Corporation.

Special discounts are available on quantity purchases by corporations, associations, educators, educational institutions, and others. For details, contact the publisher.

Please contact Alonos® through our website or via email at:
Information@Alonos.com

Suggested bibliographical reference:

Albrecht, D.J. (2018). *Organizational Design that Sticks! Multidisciplinary Approach for the Business Ecosystem.* Dallas, TX: Alonos Corporation.

Dedication

The completion of a book like this is a culmination of many years of professional development, experience, and the practice of one's profession. All of which are the reflection of both individual efforts and the support and contributions of family, friends, coworkers, and colleagues.

First and foremost I want to dedicate this endeavor to, and thank, my wonderful wife for her support and encouragement through this process. Anyone who has authored knows that writing takes place at all hours of the day and all days of the week…even over holidays. Her unwavering support encouraged the tenacity and confidence to press forward. I can never thank her enough.

Secondly I want to dedicate this book to all my past and future clients. You have my commitment to continue to pursue the practice of these disciplines and always add the most value to your business.

Contents

Author

Dr. Dale J. Albrecht is the Executive Partner and Principal Consultant for Alonos. Alonos is a business management consulting firm working with boards and executive management on organizational design and effectiveness.

Dr. Albrecht has fulfilled roles in Performance Consulting, Organizational Design & Effectiveness, Project Management, Engineering, Technical Operations, Human Resources, Education, and Change Management. He has worked in several industries including retail, manufacturing, telecommunications, medical devices, construction, and Department of Defense. He has considerable experience consulting with most corporate functional areas including supply chain, engineering, software development, sales, marketing, human resources, information technology, and service/support.

Dr. Albrecht completed his terminal degree in Business Administration with Swiss Management Center University in Zug, Switzerland. He holds a Master's in Business Administration from Columbia Southern University. He has a Bachelor's of Science Degree in Workforce Education & Development from Southern Illinois University at Carbondale, where he graduated Summa Cum Laude and a member of the Golden Key National Honor Society. He holds a certificate in Organizational Development from DePaul University. He is a certified Senior Professional in Human Resources, a SHRM-Senior Certified Professional, and an appointed Six Sigma Master Black Belt. He also holds a certificate in Project Planning, Analysis and Control from George Washington University.

Preface

Early in life I thought I was going to be an auto mechanic. I took every shop class I could in school, back in the days when vocational technical programs were offered in our secondary schools. I learned how to arc weld at 13 years old. I rebuilt my first engine at 14 years old. By the time I was 16, I was servicing the mechanical needs of a multi-crew landscaping company that my brothers and I operated. When I joined the U.S. military in my late teens I picked up training/skills in electrical systems, electronics, and telecommunications. While on deployment in Southeast Asia, I learned some building trades such as framing and drywall. A few years later, after buying a first home that was a "fixer-upper," I learned plumbing, flooring, and some basic HVAC skills. Fast forward many years to the present, and I'm often told by my wife and family that I've got just about every tool in my garage that one would need.

Acquiring a good set of tools is something that takes a great deal of time. It's not the purchase of the tools that takes time though, it's acquiring the knowledge and skills to use them effectively and appropriately. I've got the tools and the skills to tackle just about everything around the home. It stands to reason though, that I'm better at those things that I have more experience with than those that I have only done once or twice. I have extensive experience with mechanical systems, electrical systems, framing, flooring, and plumbing. I have much less experience with roofing, windows, drywall-finishing, and HVAC; with these, I prefer to call on experts. They bring a better set of tools and the expertise to wield those tools with a high degree of precision and efficiency. As much as my family enjoys watching me work through a project around the house, I enjoy watching a skilled tradesperson work their craft! The drywall finish experts probably amaze me the most. They clunk around in the dirtiest of clothes, often on stilts that would make me dizzy, and they swing trowels and floats around with both speed and finesse. They take muddy/slimy inputs and produce a finished output that is quite-frankly beautiful.

While I have enjoyed doing trades-work, it has always been my *avocation* through the years. My vocation started in communications electronics/telecommunications. During the digital transformation that started in the early 1990's, I transitioned through career roles in training, organizational performance improvement, organizational design, project management, leadership development, process systems design, and human resources.

One concept that I took with me through those career transitions was that of a "toolbox." A master-mechanic's toolbox will have hundreds of tools in it, and s/he builds knowledge and skill over time about what tools to use on what problems. Likewise, a practitioner in the human performance and organizational design space will have a myriad of tools at their disposal, that they have collected over-time, along with the experience to wield them effectively. A practitioner in this space has a toolbox full of models, templates, and analytical structures. For example, I have a folder on my computer that has thousands of templates for wall-posters that I can use to facilitate groups. Just like the master-mechanic knows when and how to apply each tool in their toolbox, a professional practitioner in human performance/organizational design knows when and how to apply each tool in their toolbox.

Another concept that I took with me through those career transitions was that of systems-thinking. The first formal exposure to systems thinking, that I recall, was in my freshman year of high school in small engine's class. With a 5-horsepower engine sitting on the bench, our teacher very clearly explained that an engine was a system of systems. An engine is a system that is designed to produce rotational energy/force. A basic design, like was sitting on the bench in front of us, was comprised of three main sub-systems: mechanical, electrical, and fuel. These sub-systems all work together in designed harmony to produce rotational energy/force. (Didn't know shop class was so intense, did you?) The engine took fuel and oxygen as it's input, used mechanical leverage and electricity to generate rotational energy as its output. I received many more lessons on systems thinking through my career transitions.

When it comes to our business organizations, we run/operate *systems*. Our companies are systems that take inputs, add productive value, and produce outputs that are consumed in the marketplace. More so, our companies are systems within systems within systems, comprising a complex nesting of systems that all work together for productivity purposes. Much like an engine, when our organizations/businesses work harmoniously, they are a work of wonder and joy. If an engine starts to sputter and skip, it no longer produces rotational energy/force effectively or efficiently. We need to troubleshoot its mechanical, electrical, and fuel sub-systems to diagnose what's not functioning properly. If a business organization starts to sputter, it no longer produces its outputs effectively or efficiently either. We need to troubleshoot its sub-systems to diagnose what's not functioning properly and to set it on proper course.

That's what I've set out to do in this book: to bring models and tools together that allow us to see the systems that are our businesses. Much like tradespeople don't *usually* design/develop their own tools, I haven't done so here either. My approach in putting this book together is to give you a tour of a skilled practitioner's toolbox, along with how to think about businesses as ecosystems. My aim being, to share with you how our firm, Alonos, approaches organizational design along with six other business performance improvement disciplines. Done with an *ecosystems* viewpoint, the application of the right mix of 7 disciplines will drive markedly higher success rates in your business initiatives!

I'm sure that many/most of us have seen those investigative news shows where they research auto repair shops that are less-than-scrupulous. It bothers us to see shops that recommend repairs that aren't needed, just so they can make money. Another thing that's bothersome is if you go to a shop to fix a problem, spend a bunch of money, and the problem is still not fixed. The same thing happens in business ecosystems all the time. Either a business goes looking for a service that they think they need, or a consulting firm sells a service without proper diagnostics. In this book, I also present an approach where business performance issues can go through an intake process and the proper disciplines can be selected and subsequently applied. I don't think it's fair/right to apply organizational design changes if organization design is not the problem. Or, if it's only part of the problem, I believe it's paramount to understand what the rest of it is…so it can be solved.

Introduction

As the title implies, this book is about engaging in *organizational design efforts that stick*. Meaning, that they are adopted by people and that they solve what they're intended to solve. You probably already know that organizational design engagements suffer from poor success rates, just like many other types of business initiatives. What is presented in this book is a way to approach business performance needs that will multiply success rates. This book focuses on organizational design, and it also focuses on six other disciplines, for a total of seven. These seven disciplines drive all business performance changes. If the goal is to improve the success rate (*stickiness*) of organizational design efforts, the other disciplines, that directly impact the performance issues, must also be examined.

Consequently, there are several key concepts and bodies of work that this book builds upon. The more familiar you are with each of these, the more value you will derive. Hopefully you will discover that this book holds value for you whether you are early in your career or a senior executive. There are several bodies of work that are essential to gaining the maximum value from this book. Seasoned business people will have exposure and familiarity with most of these.

Michael Porter's (1998) value chain model is adapted to help provide a view of our businesses as systems and to also conceptualize organizational capabilities. David Ulrich's (1987 & 1993) work, and the work of David Ulrich and Norm Smallwood (2004), on organizational capabilities is also a good basis for understanding. Peter Drucker's (1993) work about the nature of companies and their purposes in society help to frame how marketplaces function and where companies derive market value. Market value disciplines, as presented by Tearcy & Wiersema (1995) build on Drucker's work and reflect upon the "law of triple constraints," the knowledge of which will richen your reading experience. In the discipline of organizational design, Jay Galbraith's (1995) model is especially useful and is easy to understand and apply. Finally, work that was done by Chester Barnard (1948) in the middle of the last century forms much of the basis for our current body of knowledge that comprises the theory of incentives, which is critical for any business to drive performance improvement changes. If you're interested in reading on any/all of these, full bibliographical references are provided in the back of the book.

You will find, throughout this book, that what's presented is the manner in which our consulting firm engages in organizational design and the other disciplines. We have had remarkable success with this multi-disciplinary approach. It is my hope that you find this educational and that it motivates you to adopt systems thinking and use all of the 7 disciplines to drive business performance improvement. If we can help you with that journey, we would love to be able to do so.

My best in your endeavors toward improvement!

A Persistent Business Problem

A brief narrative to get started…It was the best of times, it was the worst of times; it was the opportunity of a lifetime, having finally risen to the role of CEO. The founder of the company had decided to semi-retire, and he moved to a seat on the Board as Chairman. As the new CEO, she was chosen from among four qualified internal candidates. She had 23 years with the company and her career spanned several areas including Finance, Operations, and Marketing. Her internal brand was strong, highlighted by expansive and deep working relationships in all areas of the company. She was on good footing and an excellent candidate.

She was aware of the statistics regarding success and failure rates in C-suite roles. Sources such as The Conference Board (Schloetzer, Tonello, & Larkin, 2017), Heidrick & Struggles (2015), and Harvard Business Review (Frick, 2015) report CEO turnover between 5%-18%, depending on industry. That turnover number doesn't sound bad at first, but when you couple it with some others, the situation demands more attention. Within 18 months, 2 of every 5 *new* CEO's fail. The numbers continue to get worse when expanded to include a view of executive management. CFO turnover rates average 15%, which doesn't sound too bad either, except that number is contrasted with other sources that state an average tenure of only 3-4 years. Likewise, with CIO's, turnover rates are 9-10%, but other reports state that the average tenure of a CIO is only 2-3 years.

She was also aware of the success and failure rates of initiatives. Sources like Forbes stating that 84% of digital transformation initiatives fail (Rogers, 2016). *Who isn't on a digital transformation path now?* Gartner reports that 75% of Enterprise Resource Planning

---

ERP Case Examples:

- In the first half of 2017 MillerCoors filed a $100M lawsuit against HCL over a breach of contract related to the implementation of their ERP software installation (Thibodeau, 2017).

  $100M

- In 2004 the U.S. Air Force embarked upon an ERP implementation that would replace over 200 outdated and disparate systems with an integrated and modern enterprise system. In 2013, it terminated the project after having spent $1.03 billion dollars (Kanaracus, 2013).

  $1BN

- In October of 2015, Select Comfort Corporation went live with a new ERP system. Initial announcements were all positive. Early 2017 earnings releases reported falling same store sales. ERP system issues were cited as contributing factors. The ERP project was stated to have been both behind schedule and over-budget (DePass, 2016).

(ERP) projects fail (Whyte, 2016). Price Waterhouse Coopers conducted a survey in 2014 of over 10,000 projects, and it was reported that only 2.5% of those projects achieved 100% success (Mimic, 2016). The respondents stated that over 50% of the projects were considered failures.

On her way into the CEO's position, she was given guidance by the Board. The company was healthy, a $2.8 billion revenue company, and revenue was up year-over-year for the five preceding years. Net income was proportionally growing over the same period, and the cash flow followed the same trend. The organization needed to make investments to continue to have strong performance and continue to be competitive in the future. The company needed to quickly enter the realm of e-commerce, which meant that they needed to update their ERP system. The ERP investment included financials, human capital, inventory, logistics, and field operations. One of the first things that she needed to do was to adjust their organizational structure from the top-down, adding capability in information technology, finance/accounting, operations, inventory planning, and merchandising. It was the best of times because she had a tremendous opportunity. It was the worst of times because she knew that the clock started ticking the day she stepped into the role. Her best estimate: she had 18-24 months to demonstrate positive movement toward e-commerce while ensuring that company performance continued in a positive direction.

The engagement started with a request to help with the organizational change that was needed. However, organizational efforts fair no better. Harvard Business Review reports "most studies still show a 60-70% failure rate for organizational change projects – a statistic that has stayed constant from the 1970's to the present" (Ashkenas, 2013). When that failure rate is extrapolated, it becomes daunting. According to the U.S. Census Bureau (2014), there are over 14,000 businesses in the United States that are large employers (over 1,000 employees). These businesses represent an employed population of over 60M people. If you assume that every large business goes through some organizational change every year, and you factor in the failure rates shown above, that means that **42M people** experience/witness organizational change *failures* every year! Global data is much harder to come by, but Dunn and Bradstreet (2013) reported in 2013 that there were over 225M companies worldwide, across 200 countries reporting. Applying similar assumptions and estimations, the number of people worldwide who experience organizational change failures every year would be over **1.5 Billion** out of a 7.6 Billion population.

These failure rates worried her, and many of her peers at other companies have similar firsthand experiences with these kinds of failures. The engagement moved forward with an agreement to conduct an organizational design engagement, while ensuring that everyone kept the entire ecosystem of the enterprise in mind.

Conducting an organizational change engagement, and making it successful, requires a view of the business that goes well beyond just organizational structure and change. It requires an ecosystem view.

Multi-Disciplinary Approach

Chapter Focus

There are disciplines that when combined, yield higher quality outcomes, faster execution, and generate improved sustainability. Business use of multi-disciplinary approaches lags other industries. When applied in business settings the success rate increases dramatically.

After years of wear-and-tear, your driveway needs to be redone. You believe that cement is a wonderful product that's durable and easy to maintain, so your goal is to contract to have a cement driveway installed. You get competitive bids, and you have one contractor tell you something that you didn't expect to hear, "Cement is brittle and will fall apart quickly." That's not what you expected to hear about cement, and the surprise on your face is evident, so the contractor explains. "Cement by itself is very brittle and flaky. When put together with an aggregate material, it becomes stronger and stands up well under compression, which then makes it a good paving material. When mixed with an aggregate like gravel and sand, it becomes concrete." Again, not the response you expected. I mean, come-on, they know what you're asking for right? Why the education in cement and concrete?

You tell the contractor that you thought that cement and concrete were basically the same thing, and you get the courage to tell the contractor that you're a bit annoyed by the response. "After all, you should understand that I fully intend to re-pave my driveway, and you should be quoting the right material to do so." However, the next thing that the contractor tells you is also surprising, but this time you have a different reaction:

"I tell you this because the aggregate material that you select has a big impact on the durability and longevity of your driveway. Most of my competitors don't tell you this and don't allow you to choose. They quote what's convenient for them to quote, but that's often not what's best for the life of the pavement. For example, a washed aggregate is essential, meaning that the sand and stone needs to be free of chemicals and or other fine materials because they weaken the concrete. There are a lot of contractors out there that use dirty aggregate and the pavement falls apart after just a few years. Unfortunately, we see this a lot in driveways. Roadways are inspected with tight quality controls, but most customers doing driveways don't know this information and so they don't know to ask. I want you to have a quality experience both with me as your contractor and with your driveway. Also, we need to talk about rebar…"

Your expression turns to one of interest. You've just been given some valuable information regarding your driveway project; information that will determine the strength and longevity of the project. Your expression turns to one of interest, and you look on, waiting for him to continue:

"Most contractors will put rebar in. It's the third component that's needed for strong pavement that will last. Rebar is steel reinforcement, and it needs to be properly spaced along with a good aggregate and cement. If we do all that, you'll have a nice driveway for many years. We use spacers to keep the rebar at an equal distance above the base and centered in the concrete."

This story is an illustration of a material composite that we are all very familiar with. Steel-reinforced-concrete is all around us. It is the combination of these materials (cement, aggregate, and steel) which gives it its strength and durability and make it such a useful and versatile building material. Many things are built from this composite material: roadways, bridges, multi-story buildings, parking structures, and homes. Remove any one component, or try to skimp on any component, and you end up with a weak material that fails.

There are seven business disciplines that behave the same way. Use them together, and you will have strength in results and execution of your business initiatives. Consider this the business world's equivalent of material composites: a *multidisciplinary* and *ecosystems* approach. This approach *intentionally* blends disciplines together to improve the strength of business improvement efforts and their success rates. Much like material sciences, blending business disciplines improves the chances of success and reduces the risks of failure. The use of multidisciplinary approaches has been around for a while; however, the express use in a business context has been limited. Figure 1 shows recent publications that address the subject area from 2014 through 2017. Publication volume is an indicator of where research and application are being performed, and the numbers shown highlight the multi-disciplinary focus that has been placed on education, healthcare, and engineering. The right-hand bar shows that business is under-represented. The search for publications included a comprehensive query across popular-press, opinion-editorials, and scholarly research in the English language. While not globally comprehensive, it is representative of the lack of focus that's put on multi-disciplinary approaches in business, compared to other segments.

You may recall a significant buzz about cross-functional work teams in the 1990's, and you may be thinking that this is the same thing. Rest assured, it is not. Applying multiple disciplines to business issues is much more than the use of cross-functional work teams. Using a multi-disciplinary approach is about doing multiple *types of work* together, or blending solutions, in order to derive a more powerful impact on the business ecosystem. The blending of disciplines yields

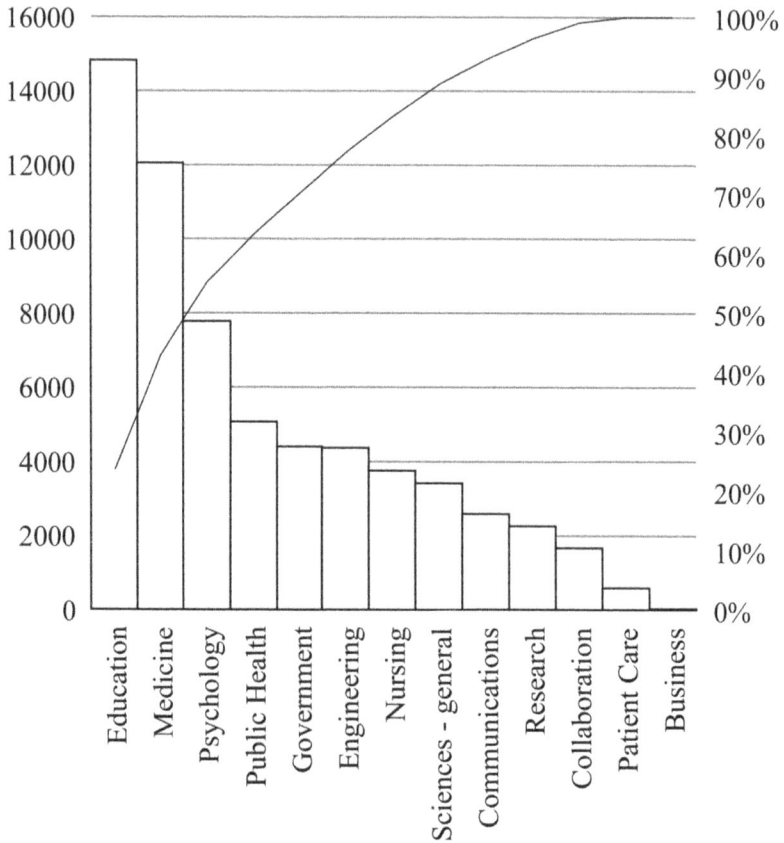

Figure 1

Multi-disciplinary Publications. The number of publications from 2014-2017 that are based on a multi-disciplinary approach, sorted by industry. Search terms were from a combination of results such as interdisciplinary, multi-disciplinary, and composites using a university library search engine that accesses 297 databases, 9,263 journals, and 39 subject guides. The same search on WorldCat yielded a similar result.

a strength in both *speed* and *quality* of business initiatives. The ability to intentionally apply the right mix of disciplines, allows companies to achieve their desired performance improvements more quickly and with higher levels of confidence. An inverse lesson has also been learned along the way: Some types of activities should be avoided by themselves. Just like using cement by itself creates a brittle output, there are disciplines, that when used by themselves, create a brittle output. Organizational design is one of them, as is evidenced by the pervasive experience of frequent designs and redesigns. Is the amount of disruption to a company's culture and performance worth a 25% chance of success? Coupling other disciplines together with organizational design can boost the success rate to over 75%!

A multi-disciplinary approach recognizes and applies systems thinking to business performance improvement. Organizational design is one discipline of seven. Others include decision rights, process design, systems, tools, people, and incentives. True business performance improvement, *that sticks*, is rarely accomplished through the execution of a single discipline. It is also rarely done by driving change in one part of the business; business improvement *that sticks* works in multiple areas to drive changes to the overall strategy and operation of the business.

It's the last few seconds of a basketball game, and the team is down by 1 point. Their star 3-point shooter is one more 3-point shot away from a personal record, and he has the ball. He puts out his best performance, making his way into shooting position, takes his record-shot, and misses. The team loses the game. The coaches are furious because they had two other players who were open and could have made a 2-point shot. Their star-shooter was thinking in a reductionist manner, and the coaches were thinking about the system. While this might be a simple illustration, the same kind of thinking occurs frequently in businesses. A functional leader proposes a project/initiative that makes a lot of sense for their operation. It has a good return on investment, and would improve the efficiency of the unit. It gets approved. The changes are made. In the process of making the changes, it has a negative effect on another department, and the company risks losing capabilities, customers, revenue, and more. While good for the function, it can have a negative impact on the company as a system.

The best reason for engaging in systems thinking is because it correlates to improved performance (Skarzauskiene, 2010). Systems thinking competencies such as process orientation, systems logic, and understanding of mental models have the highest correlation to improved organizational performance. The strength of systems thinking makes a lot of sense. Our businesses exist within many contexts (e.g. socio, economic, geo-political, technical, etc.). Within our businesses we have systems within systems within systems; a concept called nesting. The larger the business the more complex the interactions. It is paramount to be able to evaluate the interrelations, comprehend the forces that are at work on the business, and subsequently choose changes that result in improved production both in the near-term and long-term.

Systems thinking is powerful through holistic evaluation of the nested components and how they interwork with each other, and it is the basis of Peter Senge's (2006) popular book. The approach is fundamentally different than a reductionist method of thinking. Reductionism is common in western societies. Reductionist-thinking breaks down a system into its component pieces and deals with each separately. One of the unfortunate outcomes of reductionist thinking is: what may be good for a sub-system might be bad for the larger system. The most powerful outcome of systems thinking is the sustained improvement of output in the company ecosystem, and this improvement is seen in both *efficiency* and *effectiveness*. Sustained improvements are accomplished by *intentional* and *planned* selection/adjustment of *multiple variables* across *multiple disciplines*.

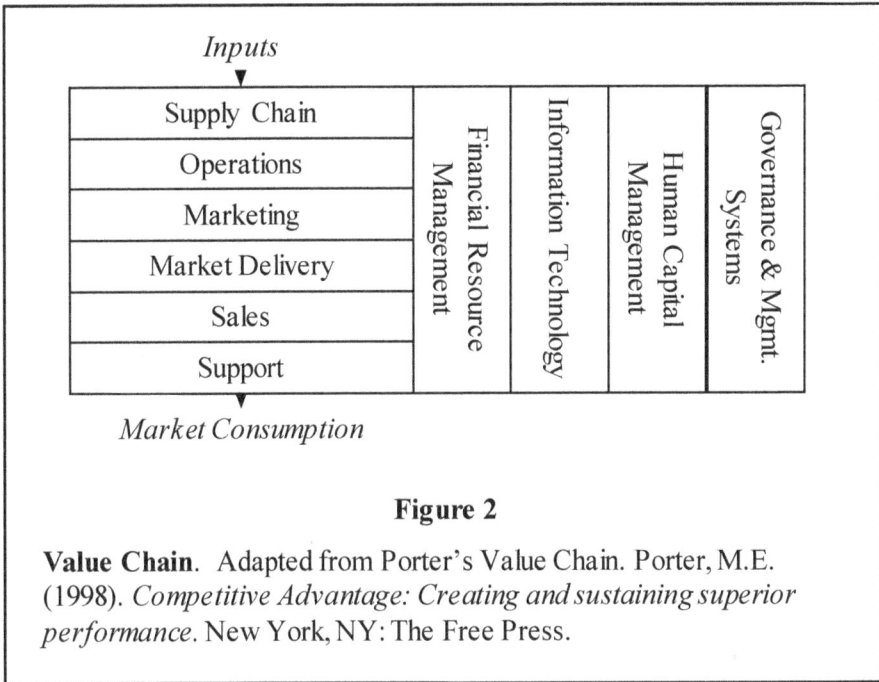

Figure 2

Value Chain. Adapted from Porter's Value Chain. Porter, M.E. (1998). *Competitive Advantage: Creating and sustaining superior performance.* New York, NY: The Free Press.

Systems thinking is also one of those things that seems to be easier said than done. Corporate career progression doesn't naturally support the development of systems thinking. Even ideal executive management teams struggle with systems thinking. The reason that teams struggle with systems thinking is that most people receive a limited breadth of *functional* experience through their careers. Even when development and career growth is planned and intentional, people will get exposure to two or three or four functional areas. That exposure is fantastic, but it still does not cover the whole of a business ecosystem. To have experienced the ecosystem of a single business, one would have to cover 10 value chain functions (Figure 2.) How long would one have to work in a value chain function to understand that function with a moderate degree of expertise? A few years? So, if you aspired to the CEO position and you wanted to work 3 years in each value chain function, you would have to invest 30 years prior to being a candidate for CEO. Investing that amount of time is really not

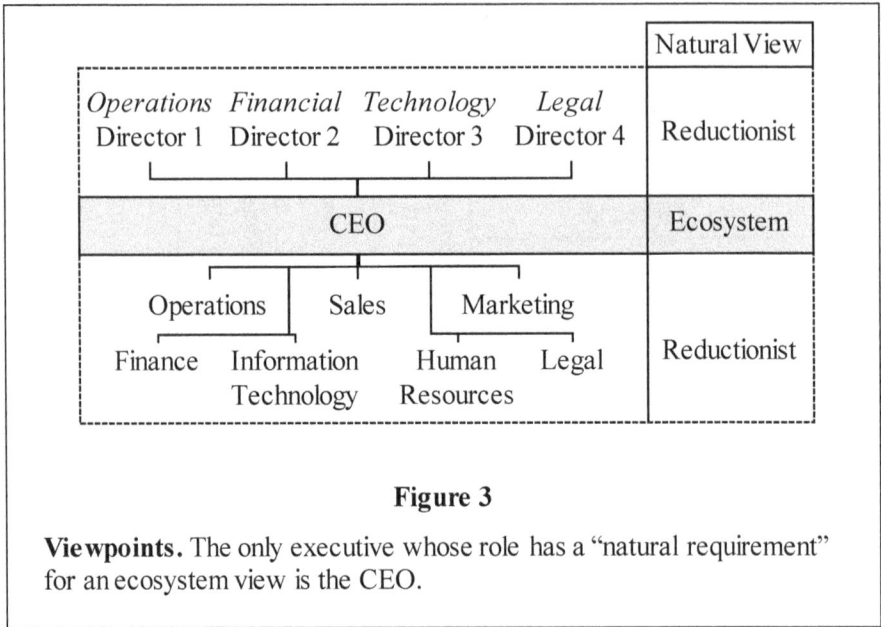

Figure 3

Viewpoints. The only executive whose role has a "natural requirement" for an ecosystem view is the CEO.

feasible, and consequently by the time people reach the executive management level, they have great depth of experience in a few of the value chain areas, but rarely more than that. Yet, executive managers are challenged to use systems thinking mental models so that their contributions are on the *whole* of the *business ecosystem*. At the same time, they are still responsible and accountable for the performance of their own function within the enterprise (unless they are the CEO.) There is often tension, and sometimes a genuine conflict of interest, between the needs of the business ecosystem and the needs of a specific value chain function. It's a challenge to say the least.

Inevitably, the <u>only</u> executive manager who is *chartered* with viewing the company in its totality, as a system, is the Chief Executive Officer (CEO) (Figure 3.) Beyond the CEO, the only other people chartered to view the company as a total system is the board. Board member selection criteria hinders systems thinking at the board level as much as it does with executive management. Boards often look for directors who have deep expertise in functional specialties like accounting, information technology, operations, legal, and marketing/sales. Reductionist thinking is one of the biggest barriers to systems thinking, for both CEO's and board members. They almost always have depth of expertise in only a few functional areas.

Figure 2 shows a depiction of a value chain, which is useful in visualizing companies as systems. All companies and organizations transform inputs into products and/or services which are consumed in the marketplace. There are direct value chain functions, which are shown on the left. These are called direct functions because they directly "touch" the inputs in the conversion. There are also indirect value chain functions, which are shown on the right. These are called indirect functions because they indirectly affect the inputs in the conversion and more-often focus on enabling the direct functions. Later in the book, this value chain model will be adapted slightly to update it for macro changes that have occurred as business has moved into the 21st century.

There are seven disciplines that are primary drivers of ecosystem performance changes. Each is used as a change-lever and impacts how the system operates; adjusting any of them will change the business ecosystem performance. Those disciplines are:

1. Organizational Structure
2. Decision Rights
3. Process Design
4. Systems
5. Tools
6. People
7. Incentives

Structure is *one* of the seven performance change levers. As stated in the previous chapter, 60-70% of organizational change projects fail. From experience, one of the most common causes of failure is that these disciplines are applied as "one-discipline engagements." For example, management works hard at coming up with what is believed to be the next-best way to structure the organization; the structure is implemented, and then performance is expected to get better. No one addresses the decision rights, processes, systems, tools, people, or incentives. A few weeks or months later the performance is still suffering, and so management goes after another change...maybe this time replacing the leader (people.) Then, a few months later when that doesn't work, management goes after an even larger organizational change. It becomes a cycle of design and re-design that doesn't deliver performance improvements.

What needs to be realized is that organizational structure is a change lever that is *interdependent* with the other 6 change levers. The organizational structure defines and *implies* roles, responsibilities, authority levels, and workflow. The organizational chart is a method of communication, to the company, about each of these. If changes are made on an **organizational** chart, but **decision/authority rights** are not defined and communicated, the company will end up with people in roles who cannot effectively execute the duties of their jobs as intended. If work **processes** aren't changed to match, the people in the new structure are left guessing about what changes in work activities management really wanted from them...who knows what kind of workflow changes will be gained, if any. If **systems** requirements and changes aren't defined to match the new organizational structure, any automated workflow, approvals, and movement of information won't occur; thereby, it would have the effect of crippling the intended authority levels and decision effectiveness of the roles. Avoid the consideration of **tools**, and people will not be able to fulfill what was a well-intended design (e.g. If a new leadership role is not enabled with the right reports and analytics, the decision quality will suffer.) Put in place a great organizational structure, and put **people** in roles that aren't a good fit for them, and performance will often drop precipitously along with the unintended development of negative team dynamics. Some would go so far as to say, 'if you put in place the right **incentives**, the

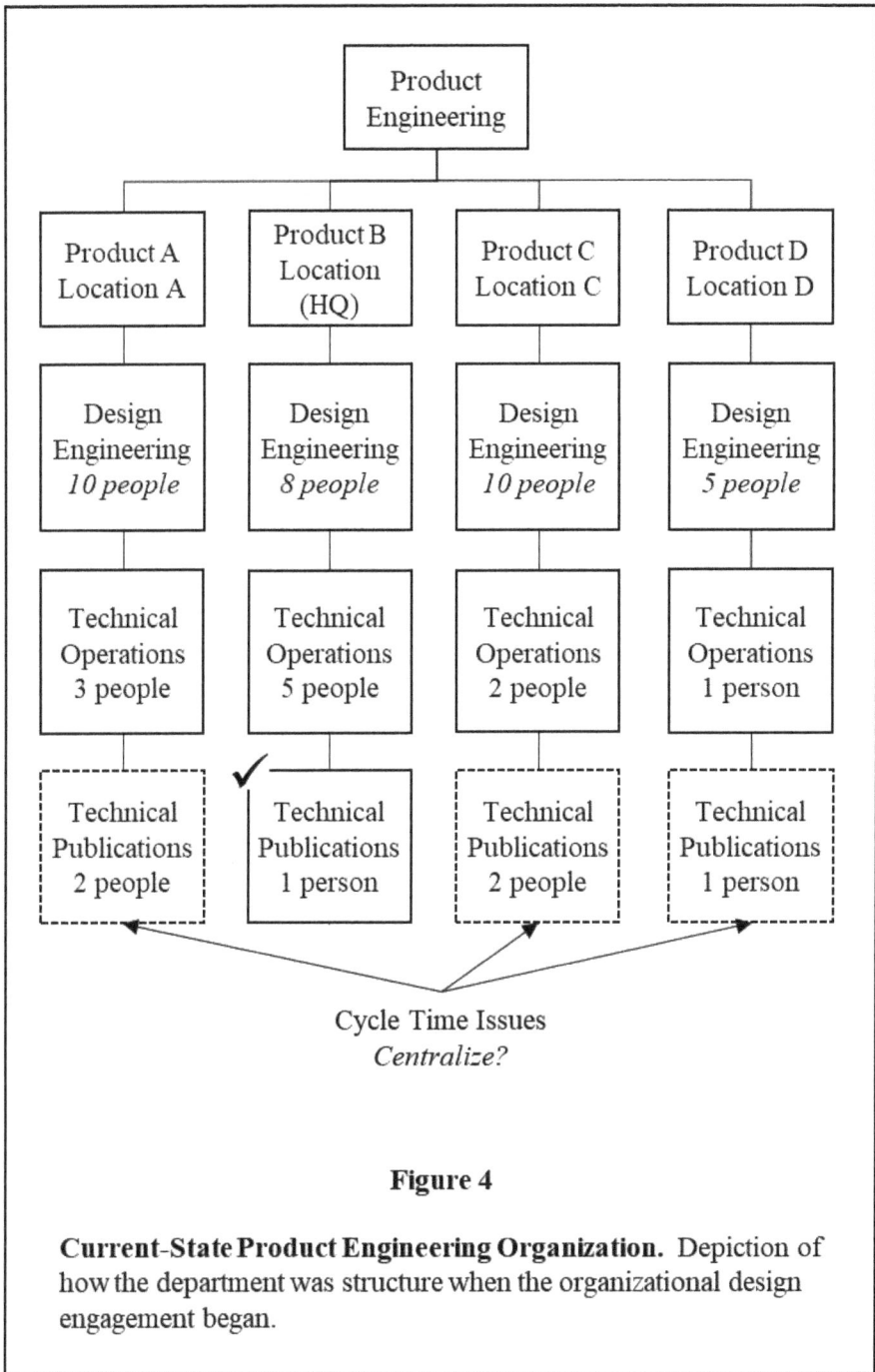

Figure 4

Current-State Product Engineering Organization. Depiction of how the department was structure when the organizational design engagement began.

rest of it will fall in place.' Without a doubt, the right incentive design is crucial for motivating both work activities and performance outcomes, but incentives work in conjunction with organizational structure and the other disciplines. Changes in **organization** structure always carry subsequent changes in **decision rights**, **processes**, **systems**, **tools**, **people**, and **incentives**. Successful organizational design requires a multidiscipline approach.

As an example, Figure 4 depicts a product engineering department. Figure 4 shows this organization as it was structured when the organizational design engagement began. The company produced four product lines, and since the products were added to the company portfolio through a series of acquisitions, each product was designed in a different location. Each product team had a consistent set of functional groups, but the resource allocation varied due to product complexity and frequency of design updates. The problem that was presented was that the department had inconsistent performance in the technical publications teams that supported each product. Product B had the best technical publications performance (indicated by the check-mark.) Product team B was able to time the releases of their technical publications to coincide with the scheduled launch dates of the products. The other three product teams (A, C, and D) had cycle time issues, with technical publications not being available until well after the product releases.

Management thought than an organizational restructure was needed. When the situation was presented, management was thinking that they might need to centralize the technical publications function to fix the timing/release issues. As depicted in Figure 5, they were contemplating moving the technical publications function to their headquarters location, and subsequently eliminating it at the other locations. A traditional approach to organizational design may have indeed yielded such a change.

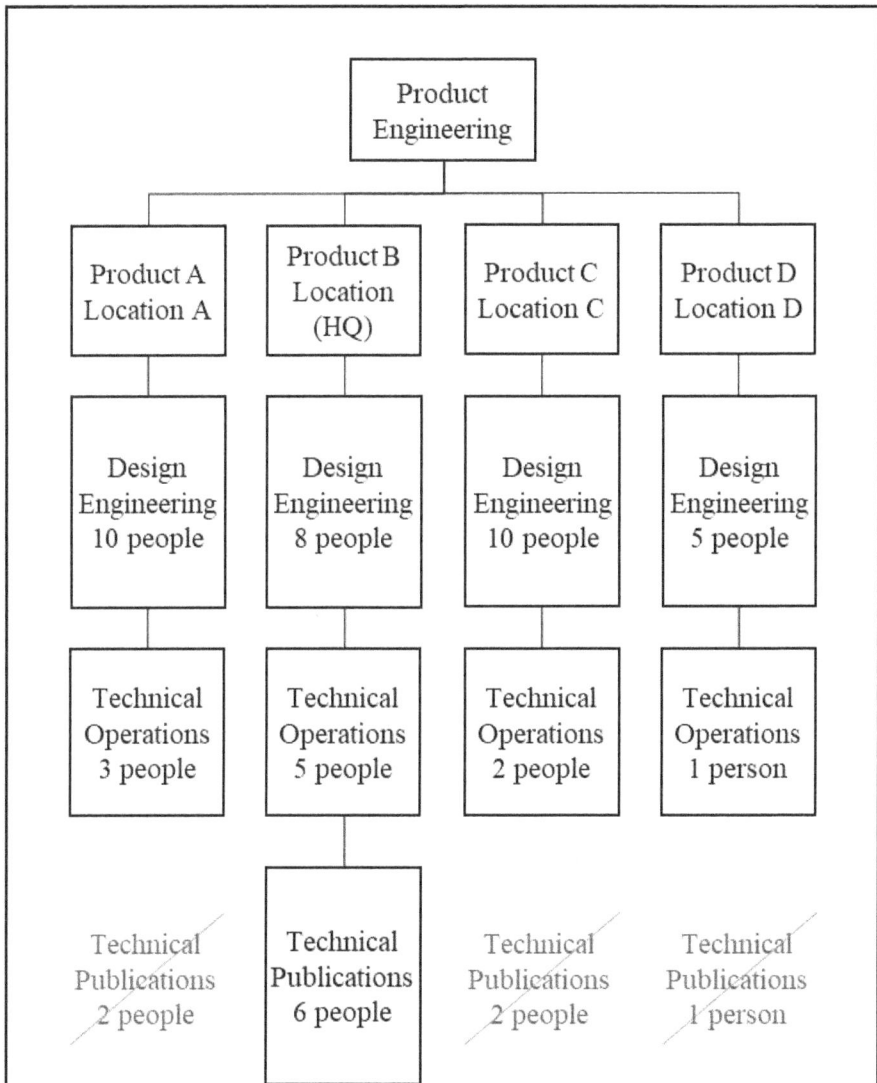

Figure 5

Organization as-proposed by management. Management's anticipated organizational changes that would fix the performance issues with technical publications.

A traditional approach to organizational design would have done the something like the following:

1. Organizational analysis to:
    a. Identify current performance gaps
    b. Define future performance criteria/design principles
2. Scoring current design against the criteria
3. Develop organizational alternatives
4. Score new alternatives against the criteria
5. Select the future state organizational structure
6. Plan and implement

There is a superior approach to organizational design, which will be described in this book. *(The model presented is called IRA-7, which is described in detail in a subsequent chapter.)* In short, multiple disciplines are applied to assess the root causes of the performance problem. Inevitably, the initial presentation of a business performance issue consists of a mix of outputs and activities, and are essentially symptoms. Symptoms need to be understood as such; they are surface indicators that need to be examined and diagnosed.

The analysis conducted with this product engineering organization used a multi-disciplinary approach and included a review of structure, decision rights, and process workflow. A simple data visualization technique was used to depict the discoveries and overlay workflow with organizational structure. Figure 6 shows what was learned. For this example, it's important to understand the role of Technical Operations when producing publications. The Technical Operations function was responsible for taking product designs and placing them into the company's configurator in their ERP system, along with generating bill-of-materials lists. This group regularly collected and reviewed engineering product designs. It made a lot of sense to have them review the content of publications, and then to load those

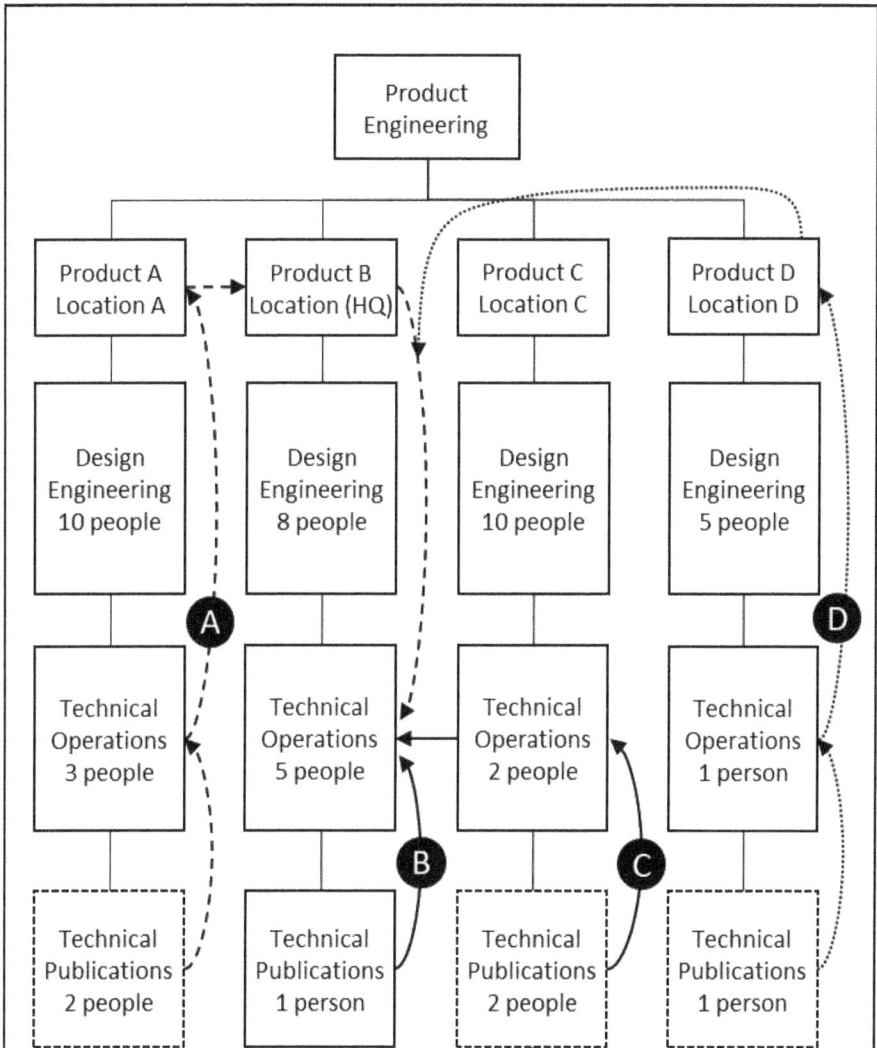

Figure 6

Current workflow. The current workflow overlaid onto the organizational structure. Shows workflow for technical publications supporting their respective product teams (A, B, C, and D.)

publications into the system for release. Workflow is indicated by the dashed-lines/arrows. Product team A moved the publications from to their technical operations function to their own product leader, who in-turn moved it to headquarters. The product leader at headquarters (Product B team leader) moved it down to their technical operations team for finalization. Contrast that flow with the workflow for Product B, who simply moved it one step for finalization. Product C also worked well, as it only required two steps. Product D followed a similar path that Product A did. This disparity in workflow between the product teams was a result of a retention of old *decision rights*. The product leaders of team's A and D held on to their approval rights even though the authority levels were pushed down through their ERP system. The system flow reflected what the company had intended. The retention of the decision rights was left over from acquisitions. The result was a workflow and process tax that was slowing things down.

The recommendation that was made is reflected in Figure 7. A discussion was facilitated with the product leaders around decision rights along with some simple workflow design changes. The outcome was an agreed upon change in workflow, which corrected the cycle time issues. In this case, no organizational changes were needed. Applying multiple disciplines yielded a better outcome for the company and its employees.

The example above is specific to that company, department, and the production of technical publications; however, the underlying characteristics of the engagement are not unique. Predetermined organizational structure changes are encountered in organizational design engagements on a regular basis. Organizational design practitioners have been taught for many decades to identify other dependent mechanisms. Organizational design publications, such as the work done by Dale (1967) and Galbraith (1995,) have correctly encouraged practitioners to identify what they call integrative mechanisms. Integrative mechanisms are those items that are needed

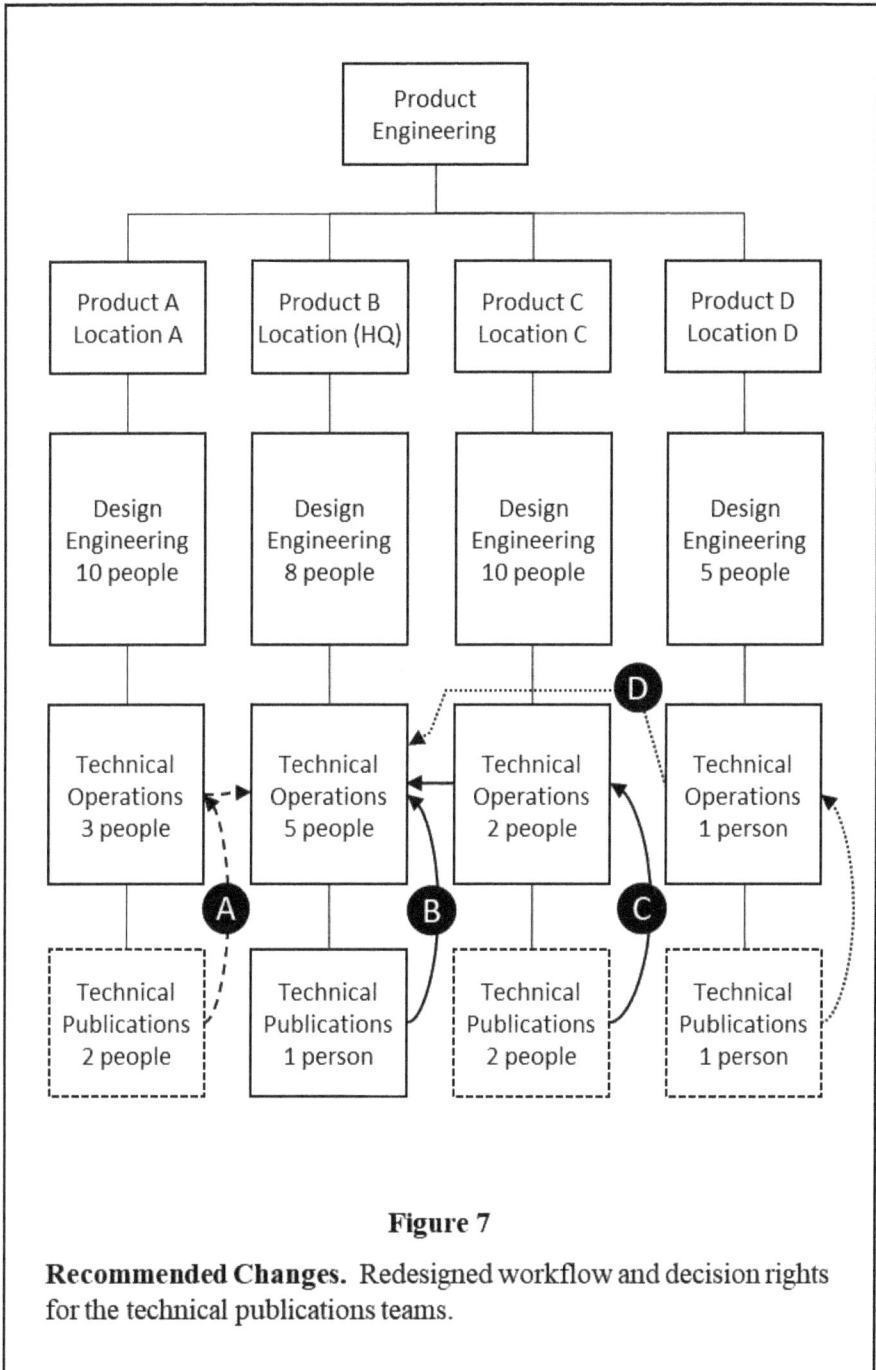

Figure 7

Recommended Changes. Redesigned workflow and decision rights for the technical publications teams.

to ensure that the newly adopted organizational structure will function as desired. However, there's a very dangerous and hidden trap with this thinking. It puts organizational structure at the focal point. An integrative mechanism is any "item" that's needed to *enable* the *organizational design*; integrative mechanisms serve the organizational design. The approach leads one to infer that organizational structure changes are always warranted. Follow this approach, and you will forever be making organizational changes.

Summary

Only a multi-disciplinary approach can deliver analyses that properly diagnose a performance problem. Only a multi-disciplinary approach will generate a change proposal that will improve the organizational ecosystem in total. This book describes a new holistic approach to driving business performance improvements. There's a focus on performing organizational design that *sticks*: that is, done in the context of interdependent disciplines…all working together to drive business performance.

Why Time Matters

> **Chapter Focus**
>
> Organizational design can be performed too frequently and too infrequently. Too often usually means that something is being missed in the analysis and design. Not often enough is an oversight by leadership that can lead to growth impediments.

Time matters in organizational design. It's a good principle to avoid frequent redesigns; frequent redesigns mean that something has been missed. On the opposite end, it's also good to ensure that organizational designs are intentional. Intentionality requires a push to design on a periodic basis that makes sense for the business. Time matters in both directions. Not designing periodically means that the business is changing without intentional thought applied to the whole of the business ecosystem; this likely means that inefficiencies are being introduced. It might come as a surprise, but *both* are equally common. Half the time, companies have been burdened by frequent redesigns and are looking to "get it right." The other half of the time, companies haven't done an organizational design process in years, and the organization has simply grown and changed over time as managers have vied for resources.

Too Often

The experience of reorganizing too often is unfortunately a common one. The situation often unfolds like this: A new leader is brought in to oversee a department/function, and they decide that a reorganization is necessary. Among the reasons are a desire to demonstrate their own leadership, assemble a team of their own advocates, demonstrate leadership-decisiveness, and invoke changes in the new organization that will help improve performance. The organizational changes are made, and the new leader has checked-off their first major change initiative. The leader feels good about the people that they're surround by now, and the new leadership team moves forward. However, root cause diagnoses are often left undone, so the leadership team is unaware of the causes of performance issues. Even though the organization structure has been adjusted, there is minimal net-effect on performance because root causes are not understood and the other six disciplines have not been invoked to make ecosystem changes. Consequently, this can cause and perpetuate subsequent organizational structure redesigns. When performance improvement is not realized, the business goes back to organizational structure changes again and often includes leadership changes. In situations like these, employees end up experiencing reorganizations too often.

While organizational changes may indeed be warranted, the true motivation of this approach is not business performance improvement, it's the needs of the individual leader. This leadership approach places the needs of the individual leader above the needs of the business ecosystem. Organizational structure becomes a convenient reason for a lack of performance. Changing the organization provides evidence that executives have acted. The conclusion that's often made is that either the change was not enough or the wrong people are in place, which in-turn causes another organizational change. Once in this pattern of frequent organizational redesigns it becomes harmful to the company's performance and degrades the culture.

Mature system-thinking leaders realize that the structure of the organization is only one part of the business ecosystem. To drive an improvement in performance, they know that changes need to be implemented to enable the *system* to generate products or services more effectively and efficiently. Organization may indeed be one of the levers, but it is also *not* the only one that needs to be pulled. *Further planning is needed to solve for the other necessary changes in the eco-system that generate improved performance and avoid frequent redesigns.*

Another common reason for frequent reorganizations is avoiding the reality of our own complexities. Once a company reaches a certain size, operating within an organizational-matrix is a real phenomenon and frankly a necessity. In very large enterprises, the matrix takes on multi-dimensional complexity and even the term "matrix" is insufficient to describe how the organization operates; it could better be described and visualized as a cube. (Since matrix is a commonly used term, we'll use it here to represent multi-dimensionality.) A company that is in this stage must be able to manage in multiple directions at the same time or else one aspect of performance will be optimized and another sub-optimized. For those who don't address the matrix intentionally and systemically, organizational structure changes become a regular occurrence. When performance in one aspect dips, someone proposes a reorientation of organizational structure to correct it. The changes are made, and then several months later performance dips in the other aspect. Someone proposes a reorganization to correct it, and the cycle begins again. The following is an example with a sales team:

This sales team had restructured three times in two years. The team was historically a geographically aligned team with formal territory definitions. They tried a *product* structure in addition to the *geographic* structure, where a smaller product sales team was put in place to service larger customers with more complicated and extended sales processes. The latest restructuring included an investment in a new/additional sales team for premium products which accounted for a 20% increase in headcount. They were using structure to reorient themselves to their own matrix, bouncing between a geographic, customer, and product view. Each restructure optimized one aspect and subordinated the others.

Through analysis and investigation, it was learned that the company had grown over a period of about 10 years by continued development of their product portfolio. Their market-entry, 10 years earlier, was in the "low-end," and they subsequently developed product in the "medium" space, and then more recently the "high-end" *(Think good, better, best. The margins followed the product tiering, making the high-end products the most profitable.)* The high-end products were introduced two years prior to the restructuring mentioned here, which is when there was a renewed sense of urgency around the sales force's execution. After the two prior reorganizations, the prevailing view was that the sales force was not capable selling high-end products; high-end products warranted a different *value-based* sales method. They thought they had a talent/skill problem; consequently, they had put in place a new sales team as an overlay. This new team was great at selling the high-end products, but the company soon realized that the resultant cost-of-sales was too high. Investigation revealed things about the eco-system that had not been considered:

- The sales methods, tools, and incentives had been established around the company's market entrance, which was low-end products. They had not been revised to fit the new product tiering and mix.
- The sales methods were transaction based and the tools/metrics drove quantity of sales calls.
- Sales incentives were built to maximize call frequency and customer contacts. This worked well, even through the mid-tier of products, because customers more naturally understood the value of the products, and the customer engagement was mostly transactional. The advent of high-end products required more consultation.

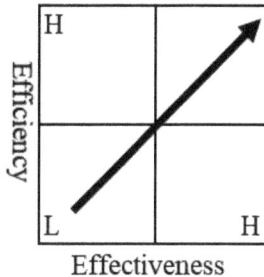

Figure 8

Effectiveness and efficiency grid. Matrix depicting the movement that an organization strives to achieve to be optimally effective and optimally efficient at delivering goods and services on behalf of the firm.

Applying a multidisciplinary view to the ecosystem, other changes were proposed, not just the structure. The company decided to return to a geographic structure with changes to sales methods, tools, and incentives. They executed the changes over a period of 18 months, and the sales force was able to successfully sell high-end products in a consultative manner.

The issue of redesigning too often, due to the complexity of the matrix, is usually first experienced at mid-market sized companies. Its resolution is essential for continued growth with healthy margins; not doing so causes margin erosion. Once a large company, managing this kind of complexity becomes a constant duty.

Not Often Enough

You've probably heard the saying "time heals all wounds." That saying is used when referring to healing the human body or emotions. Over time, physical and emotional wounds will *for-the-most-part* heal themselves. However, when it comes to organizational health, the opposite is true. When organizations are left to simply evolve on their own, time wounds most organizations.

Companies strive for optimal effectiveness and efficiency, shown as a simple 2 X 2 grid in Figure 8. Companies strive to move into the upper right-hand quadrant. Such an illustration is great if the company is stagnant, but viewing companies as stagnant is not anyone's reality. The reality is that our businesses are always either growing or shrinking.

Assume an organization is both optimally-effective and optimally-efficient today. They are operating in the upper right-hand quadrant shown in Figure 8. Over the next 5 years the organization is successful and grows at an 8% compounded annual growth rate (CAGR.) Eight percent per year seems manageable, right? At that rate of growth, a $500M company turns into a $735M company. A reasonable 8% annual growth rate is something very different at the end of a 5-year cycle. Over the course of 5 years, the company has experienced a compounded growth of **_47%_**! Stop and think about that for a second: An 8% annual growth rate yields a 47% compounded gain over a five-year period.

What are the ecosystem implications of allowing the business to organically evolve over that period of time? Evolving and scaling organically can work in some cases, but in others it is woefully insufficient. Departments and functions that process volume-based transactions have the most success scaling-up organically. For example, in the accounting department of a company that experienced a similar growth rate as mentioned, invoice processing, billing/receivables, and payables grew proportionally to the growth of the business over that 5-year period. The changes in accounting were volume-based, and the department added personnel, software licenses, and tools (e.g. computers, scanners, fax machines, file cabinets) that allowed them to complete the higher number of transactions. Resources were added to the billing, accounts payables, and accounts receivables departments. There was no need for fundamental changes in the accounting department.

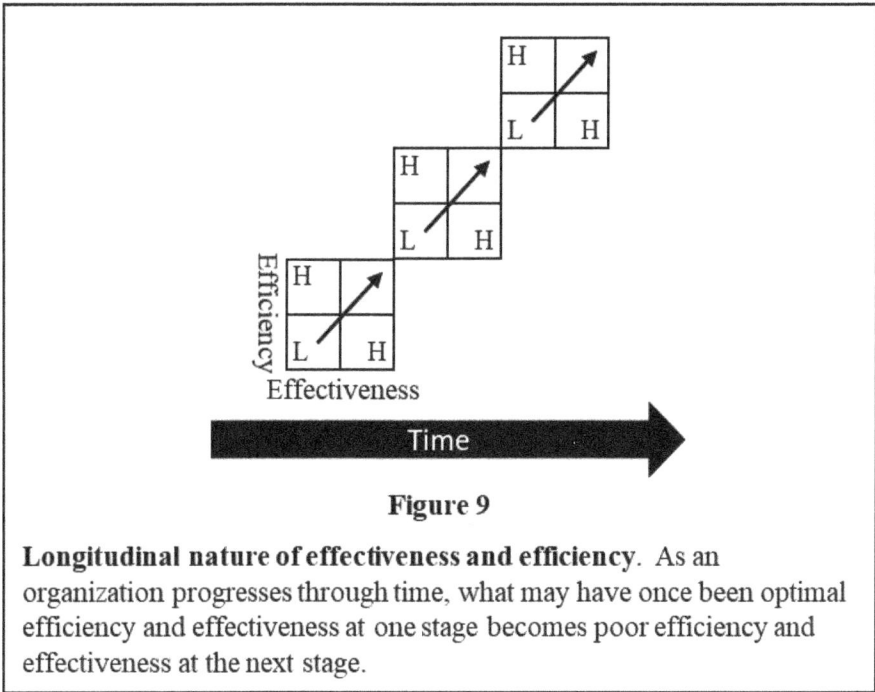

Figure 9

Longitudinal nature of effectiveness and efficiency. As an organization progresses through time, what may have once been optimal efficiency and effectiveness at one stage becomes poor efficiency and effectiveness at the next stage.

There are other departments and functions that, when faced with the same business growth, require changes in *organizational capabilities*. They quickly find themselves no longer effective or efficient at their work. As Figure 9 illustrates, what was high efficiency/effectiveness at one growth stage becomes low efficiency/effectiveness at the next. Departments and functions that require growth and development of new/additional capabilities find themselves struggling to deliver the outputs needed to enable the business to grow further. When these are left to "evolve" over time they can become barriers for the company; eventually, any department like this will become a limiting factor. The organization must intentionally design and build toward optimal efficiency and effectiveness at each stage.

At the same company, from its inception through the $500M point, human resources (HR) reported to the CFO. This is common in small companies, as the nature of the work in HR is highly transactional at the early stages of a business' lifecycle. The HR work consisted of hiring, employee records, payroll, and administration paperwork. As this company grew from $500M to $800M their needs changed dramatically. The growth caused the company to expand their operating units so that they could provide additional services to the marketplace. Where they had gone to market through one operating unit in the past, they now expanded to seven operating units, each with its own sources of revenue and each with a full profit and loss (P&L).

The impact of the business changes meant that the company now needed many more *capabilities* from HR. Benefits administration needed to evolve to include third party management of a brokerage along with benefit plan designs, which took the company away from a fully insured plan toward a partially self-insured plan. A full compensation function needed to be developed which addressed pay-for-performance, planned merit cycles, internal and external pay equity, and strategically aligned incentive plans. In addition, local and state contracts required sophistication in compensation analyses, design, and compliance. The company's hiring methods also needed dramatic change. The employee base grew from 450 to 1,200 in the same period, and the labor market became more competitive. No longer were referrals and signage enough to bring-in the talent that the company needed. They also needed a web/social media presence, an applicant tracking system (ATS), and a formal on-boarding process that varied by type of role. The CFO, while highly astute at accounting and finance, was not the HR leader that the company now needed. What was an effective and efficient HR department five years earlier, was now an ineffective and inefficient function that was impeding the company's growth. Similar capability deficiencies were identified in several of the major functions for the company, including operations, supply chain, transportation & logistics, and sales.

The company had waited too long to address organizational structure changes and overall organizational capabilities that were needed to continue to be competitive. Once they saw the impact it was having on their business ecosystem, they made the necessary organizational structure changes and investments in capabilities. Those investments resulted in the development of new capabilities, which allowed them to push those departments back into the upper right-hand quadrant: being both efficient and effective. Through the process, they realized that this was a stage…a springboard to the next level of performance, and that they would need to do this again.

Needed changes like the ones described above un-fold over and over across industries and company types. In growth situations, it is a common and expected occurrence to go through *capability changes*. The business functions/departments most susceptible to capability changes include operations, engineering, research and development, human resources, information technology, supply chain, marketing, sales, and engineering. Where functional departments have been left to evolve on their own, those departments can end up being wounded by time, to a point where they become an impediment to the company's progress.

Summary: The Longitudinal & Systemic Nature of it All

- When was the last time your company did an organizational design review in the context of *needed* capabilities?
- How often do you believe you should do this?

They're simple questions, but their answers reveal what *should be* the longitudinal nature of organizational design. The review against *capabilities* reveals what should be a *business ecosystem approach*, examining the whole of the business to drive changes to the system that will generate the desired performance improvement. Both ends of the timeline are damaging from an organizational structure standpoint. Redesigning too frequently is harmful because it misses the ecosystem itself, and redesigning too infrequently is harmful because it misses developing critical organizational capabilities that could impede further growth.

Establishing a Base for Organizational Design

Chapter Focus

This is a "watersheds" chapter, establishing some foundational views that every practitioner should consider as they conduct organizational design engagements. This chapter grounds the practitioner in the business of running a business and delivering market value. This grounding is essential for organizational design engagements to contribute to business success.

There are a few foundational considerations that form the basis for organizational design engagements; these are principles that need to be followed in organizational design. Following these helps to ensure that organizational design engagements are focused on the *ecosystem* of the business, and that they employ multiple disciplines which promote improved business performance.

Value Focused

The first item of note, in for-profit companies, is delivering economic market value. A company exists to deliver goods and services that customers will purchase, and it is a company's aim to position itself in the market so that a customer will choose to buy from them versus a competitor or another substitute. *Organizational efficiency* is a company's ability to deliver products and/or services to the marketplace using the least amount of raw material and resources.

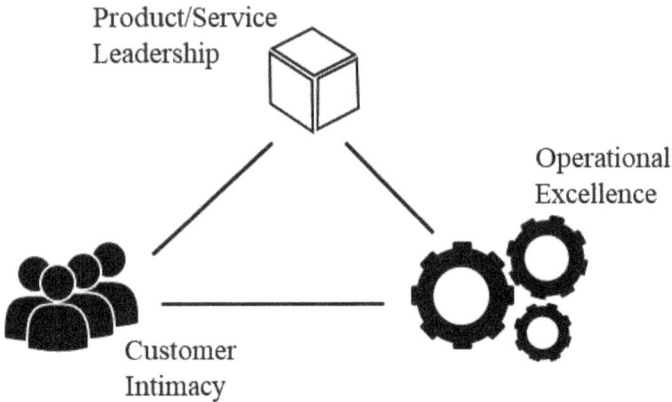

Figure 10

Value disciplines. Adapted from Tearcy, M. & Wiersema, F. (1995). *The Disciplines of Market Leaders*. New York, NY: Harper Collins Publishers, Inc.

Organizational effectiveness is a company's ability to deliver products/services competitively with quality, timeliness, and repeatability.

Organizational design should be undertaken with a solid understanding of a company's business, market positions, customer base, and value proposition. One of the easiest value proposition models to remember is the one developed by Tearcy & Wiersema (1993). Figure 10 shows this model, which depicts three aspects of differentiation. The premise of the model is that all companies lead with one of the three, and the others take second and third place. All companies have a mixture of all three aspects that they bring into the marketplace. A company chooses how to deploy resources to promote their primary leadership position in the marketplace as either being a product leader, customer intimate, or operationally excellent/efficient.

The manner in which a company chooses to differentiate itself will be reflected in everything that it does: strategy, organizational structure, decision rights, processes, systems, tools, people, incentives, allocation of operational and capital expenditures, and metrics. The chosen value proposition of the company will permeate everything. Understanding this principle enables the practitioner to guide teams to create organizational alternatives that align with the company's value proposition.

Take for example an IT services outsourcing company that wins contracts because of their ability to place solutions teams on-site with their business clients. Local teams engage their clients on a day-to-day basis and have intimate knowledge of their client's business. One of the organizational characteristics that would be present in this IT outsourcing company would be decentralized sales and solutions teams. Recommending organizational solutions that risk this fundamental principle would put the company's value proposition at-risk.

It is difficult to over-emphasize the point about being value-focused. Unfortunately, there are far too many cases of organizational design practitioners who are not able to discern a company's market-value propositions. There are many executive leaders who struggle to do the same, or simply neglect to perform the review. Famous struggles with value proposition in the recent past and in the public press include Yahoo!, Danier Leather, Sears, and RadioShack (Rosa, S., 2013; Nadeau, M & Dedijer, J., 2017). As organizational design efforts are undertaken, to improve efficiency and effectiveness, it is paramount that the company's market value proposition be clearly understood by all internal and external resources who will work on the engagement.

Business Capability

Organizational design efforts should be approached from the standpoint of *capabilities*. This may seem obvious, but it is often difficult to get a leadership team to agree on a list of *capabilities* that provide the company a unique value proposition in the marketplace. Business capabilities flow from the company's value proposition; the right capability mix needs to be in place so that the company can process inputs and deliver products/services into the marketplace at a quality and price that customers will purchase. A capability discussion will usually start with a historical view of what *has been* the company's capability mix; however, the discussion needs to move toward a view of what *will-be* the capabilities that the company will use to continue to differentiate itself.

There's a concept called "creative destruction" that was put forward by Joseph Schumpeter in the early 20th century (McCraw, 2009). The essence of creative destruction is that capitalistic economies live on a creation and disruption cycle. As new technologies and innovations come to market, old ones are displaced. The creation and disruption cycle should be viewed as a hallmark strength of the capitalistic system. It is the essence of opportunity – find something to disrupt with a new innovation and you can create market value and maybe even a whole business or industry.

History is full of examples such as electricity, rubber, concrete, steel, gunpowder, and transistors. Modern examples include things such as the personal computer, mobile/cell telephones, smartphones, and cloud computing and storage. One can easily argue that social progress depends on creative destruction. Some additional (potential) examples, that are still developing, include genomics, digital currencies, artificial intelligence, 3D printing, and autonomous driving. Just like creative destruction propels society forward, it does the same for organizational capability.

The most challenging aspect of internal capability analysis is getting the leadership team to examine external changes with a view toward organizational capabilities. Organizational capabilities must first be identified and defined in a systematic manner so they can subsequently be challenged. The outcome being that the mix of internal

Figure 11

Interdependent Organizational Constructs (IOC's). The combination of these three constructs is what fills-out a firm's strategy and allows it to translate strategy into operational plans and objectives.

capabilities can be adjusted through planned initiatives and projects, and they can be actively managed.

Engaging in this internal "creative destruction" is made more difficult because it is human nature to become "comfortable" and "relaxed" as we experience success. We have a tendency to lean on techniques and approaches that we believe have generated our success, and we become comfortable in our beliefs. To ensure long term viability of our businesses in today's markets, we need to build-in an explicit mechanism that promotes "creative destruction." Formalized organizational capability analyses should be performed regularly, in conjunction with the business' strategic planning process, and it is recommended that this be externally facilitated. An external facilitator brings needed neutrality and objectivity for assessing a business' organizational capability mix.

The interactions of product/service innovation, value discipline orientation, and organizational capability are what differentiates a company. As Figure 11 depicts, each of these are *interdependent organizational constructs*; one is *not* dependent/subordinate to another. The three interact dynamically to deliver either success or failure in the marketplace. It is imperative that the interaction of these three be fully understood as a basis for organizational design. Discerning these and proactively managing them are also a leadership imperative. The moment that a leadership team allows new development, growth, and/or removal of an organizational capability it changes is value orientation and an aspect of the products/services it delivers to the marketplace.

As a basis for organizational design, there are three aspects of *changing* capabilities that always need to be explored: creation, growth, and removal. <u>All organizational design changes adjust organizational capability</u>, but only those done explicitly derive *desired* capability changes. When not addressed explicitly, organizational design changes often have detrimental and unintended effects to organizational capability.

When Re-Designing is Essential

Business growth is a common cause for organizational redesign. Growth over time was the basis for the previous chapter on "why time matters." This section looks deeper at business growth and how it drives organizational redesign. To start, it helps to understand where the business growth is coming from.

Applying a tool like Ansoff's matrix, as shown in Figure 12, is very helpful to understand the basis for growth. The vertical axis is either new or existing products or services. The horizontal axis is either new or existing markets. The type of growth represented by each quadrant will be explored along with the potential implications to organizational capabilities – and in-turn the potential implications to organizational structure.

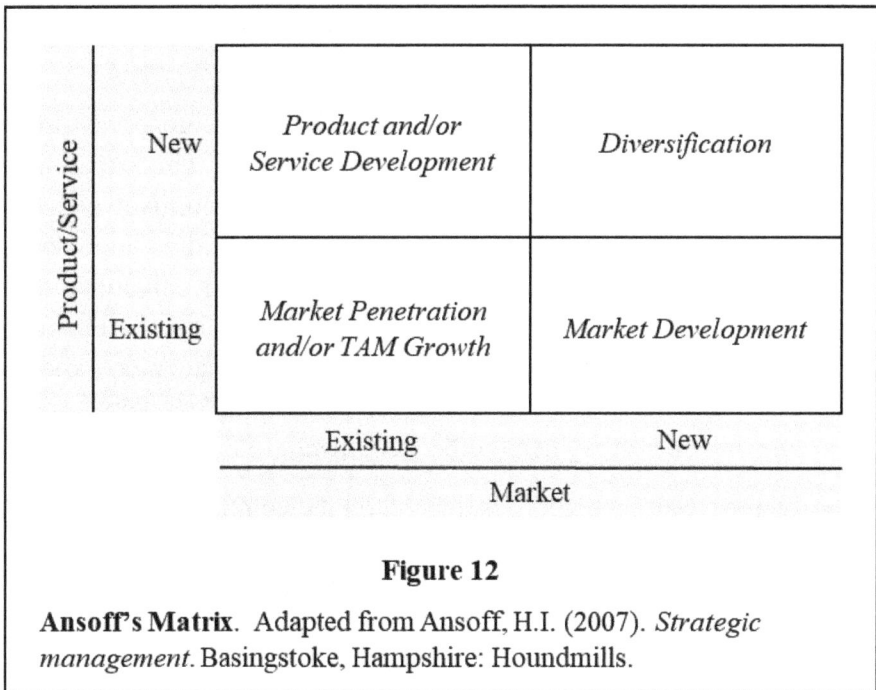

Figure 12

Ansoff's Matrix. Adapted from Ansoff, H.I. (2007). *Strategic management.* Basingstoke, Hampshire: Houndmills.

When a company's growth strategy consists of driving **existing products/services** into an **existing market** (a market that the company currently operates in,) this is referred to as a *market penetration* strategy (bottom-left quadrant.) "Market penetration" may not be the best choice of terminology, as it implies growing a company's percent of market share. It is possible to increase top-line revenue if the Total Available Market (TAM) is growing, even if the company maintains market share. If the TAM is growing rapidly enough, a company may also increase top-line revenue while losing market share. The essence of this strategy is that the company is driving for growth using an existing product/service portfolio in a market that it currently does business.

This growth strategy may require organizational design and capability changes such as:

- **Marketing**: Marketing will need to be able to generate traffic for sales, market interest, and brand identity. This capability-need will have impacts to advertising, brand management, creative, sales enablement, and events. It could be a matter of scaling-up capacity in each of these areas, but small companies may need to refine capabilities. For example, a small business may not have an explicit focus on brand management, and as they grow, even with a market penetration strategy, brand management may need to be formalized.

- **Sales**: Sales capabilities depend on the company's go to market approach. An outside/direct sales approach will need improved ability to reach and impact a larger number of customers and have a greater impact on current customers. While this may be a scaling-up of the number of sales people, it may also mean the addition of new sales capabilities. For example, a small company may have the sales leader manage territories, call planning, metrics, and incentives. As the small company grows, they may need to add a sales operations capability that will handle these activities.

- **Supply Chain**: Supply chain capabilities include distribution, inventory management, traffic management, and supplier capacity planning. Even though a market penetration strategy keeps the business within an existing marketplace, each of these supply chain functions will be impacted by increased volume. The increased volume of activity may mean changes in capabilities and structure for sourcing, inventory, merchandising, geographic information systems, and analytics. For example, it is typical for small businesses to outsource the movement of their own goods, using existing carrier networks for delivery. Volume increases could trigger economies of scale where it's more efficient for a business to lease dedicated routes between cities and even purchase their own branded containers. An event like this could change the capabilities from needing to order space on a brown truck to a formal traffic/logistics function.

- **Manufacturing, Production, and Operations**: A market penetration strategy would mean increase volume for the production functions. Capacity increases in production can mean additional capital expenditures even in a situation with existing products and an existing market. For example, a business that produces durable goods, expanding in its current market may require additional manufacturing capacity beyond its current plant structure. They could either increase capacity at their current plant, or they might explore establishing a new plant in a different part of the country. Building a new plant would give them added capacity, and it would give them back-up capabilities too. Or, a third option could be to outsource a portion of their manufacturing need. Any option would require capability changes in manufacturing operations, and potentially organizational structure changes.

- **Information Technology (IT)**: In a market penetration strategy, IT can still be impacted in many ways. The company's IT system architecture would need changes to accommodate a larger company footprint, new locations, and increases in production capacity. New capabilities may be driven by new suppliers, new outsourcers, new facilities, growing partnerships, and density of presence…to name a few.

- **People**: A market penetration strategy's volume increases brings with it a natural increase in the number of people associated with each of the above areas. Functions and departments will grow through the addition of new employees.

Depending on the approaches taken above, new resources may also be provided through staff-augmentation, outsourcers, and other third-party providers. In addition to number of people, new talent categories that drive new organizational capabilities could also be a requirement. Finally, on top of it all is a need to develop the super-structure of the company as it grows and to ensure a robust leadership team and talent pipeline.

When a company's growth strategy consists of driving **existing products/services** into **new markets**, this is referred to as a *market development* strategy (bottom-right quadrant). The essence of this strategy is that the company is driving growth using an existing product/service portfolio in a new market that it does not currently do business. This growth strategy can require organizational redesign and capability changes such as:

- **Marketing**: Even though traffic generation for sales is always the aim of marketing, other markets can behave dramatically differently. Marketing will need to develop the capability to generate awareness and interest in the new market. Marketing will also need to answer questions about the business' products/services related to homogeneity and adaptation. Does the company need to make product/service adaptations? What pricing structure fits the new market's supply and demand constraints and generates a demand level that the business can effectively meet? Does the company need to make advertising and go-to-market adaptations? If new markets require adaptation, then capability changes will be needed in branding, advertising, creative, sales enablement, and events. This may mean new field marketing teams, multi-lingual and multi-cultural resources, and new agency partnerships.

- **Sales**: When developing a new market, the impact to sales capabilities depends on the company's go-to-market approach.

An outside/direct sales approach will require physical presence in the market. This will mean hiring a sales force, establishing new territories based on expected volumes, and sales incentive plan development. Sales force enablement will benefit from the fact that the business is selling existing products and services, even if they are adapted. Resources should be available that can be modified to the new market versus having to development them from scratch; however, there will be a new capability required that addresses sales enablement in an on-going basis.

- **Supply Chain**: The supply chain must be able to move the goods/service to the new market and subsequently be able to move them to their points of distribution, sales, and consumption. Supply chain capabilities include distribution, traffic lanes/management, inventory management, and supplier capacity planning. Market development will require new physical presence for the movement of goods and services. This can be achieved through internal development, contracting, partnering, and joint ventures. Each approach brings with it a separate set of capability needs for sourcing, inventory, merchandising, geographic information systems, analytics, and overall supply chain management.

- **Manufacturing, Production, and Operations**: A market development strategy requires that the company solve for how/where it produces and how it gets products/services into the new market. Manufacturing and production in a new market can mean additional capital expenditures to establish production capability in that market. A company may also choose to ship product into the new market from an existing production facility, or they may choose to work through third parties to establish capability. All options require capability changes in manufacturing operations, and potentially organizational structure changes that provide the required management super-structure. Establishing a new company-owned manufacturing facility in a new market requires a vastly different organizational structure than partnering with a co-packer or co-manufacturer in a new market.

- **Information Technology**: New facilities, partners, third parties, and geographically dispersed employees all have significant impact to IT requirements and capabilities. System architecture changes will be needed to accommodate a larger company footprint. New equipment providers may need to be sourced along with establishing the capability to service the new IT infrastructure. The IT capabilities that will need to be addressed include design, development, quality assurance, deployment, integration, configuration, and support.

- **People**: People capabilities follow the changes needed in each of the above areas. These could include new talent/skills that the organization has not previously had, and it can also mean an increase in the number of people associated with each of the above areas. Acquiring talent in the new market will be the first need, and then quickly following, all other human capital management duties will also be needed. Leadership development within the new market should take a priority early-on in market development, because the needed leadership qualities may change quickly as the business grows and matures. Being able to rely on a leadership bench helps provide growth stability.

When a company's growth strategy consists of driving **new products/services** into **existing markets**, this is referred to as a *product/service development* strategy (top-left quadrant). The essence of this strategy is that the company is driving growth using an existing market presence to introduce an expanded product/service portfolio. This growth strategy usually requires organizational capability changes and organizational redesign work, such as:

- **Marketing**: Again, traffic generation for sales is always the aim of marketing. With a strategic focus on new products, marketing may need additional capability in the areas of pricing and product management; however, product management may also sit within product development and/or operations. Wherever the capability resides, it is the responsibility of this function to plan and manage the product lifecycle. Product Life Cycle Management (PLCM) is likely being performed with existing product strategies; however, when new products become the focal point of a company's strategy, the capability for PLCM becomes paramount because PLCM acts as the company's coordinating function for product launches. PLCM is always important, but it becomes increasingly critical when a company is pursuing an expansion of product offerings. For example, new products will mean that marketing will need to prepare sales with additional collateral, and there may also be branding and advertising implications.

- **Sales**: New products in existing markets means that sales will need to represent a broader product/service portfolio. Depending on the portfolio implications, sales may need to be approached differently with a new capability such as solutions selling compared to transactional/feature based selling. A shift such as this may have implications on sales methodology, automation tools, incentives, and skills training. In more substantial changes, it may also require wholesale changes in talent makeup.

- **Supply Chain**: With new products in existing markets, it will be necessary to do both a supply-side and distribution-side examination of the supply chain. This can begin by looking at supplier capabilities. New products will often require additional/different suppliers and consequently improved supplier management capabilities for the company.

Distribution, traffic, and logistics may also be impacted, especially for those companies producing products (versus services.) Physical products are often facility/location dependent requiring capital investments. The development of new products may mean new or expanded facilities, either has implications to the capabilities of those facilities, distribution, and organizational structure.

- **Manufacturing/Production/Operations**: New products mean new production capabilities. This can require both operational and capital investments. In manufacturing, it means new lines or adaptations of existing lines. The company may utilize existing facilities to product the new products, but that will mean a reallocation of physical resources. Even if the same manufacturing lines can be used with minimal tooling changes, making the changeover requires resources and reduces capacity that could be used for other products. The full capability and capacity impacts will need to be examined, and these may have organizational impacts, especially if it means new shifts, expanded facilities, or new facilities.

- **Information Technology**: System architecture changes to accommodate a larger product portfolio include not only increases in capacity, but also new product bills-of-materials, system configurations, pricing tables, workflows, and much more. Many of these new capabilities have a distributed effect in companies, not only impacting the information technology department, but also impacting other departments such as supply chain, accounting, and operations.

- **People**: One really cannot escape the people capability implications of any of the strategic approaches. People capabilities follow the changes needed in each of the above areas. The fact that this strategy leverages an existing market for the company should limit changes to those that are mostly field-based.

When a company's growth strategy consists of driving **new products/services** into **new markets**, this is referred to as a *diversification* strategy. The essence of this strategy is that the company is driving growth through new markets while simultaneously introducing new products/services. The degree of diversification is in-part determined by the degree of departure from current types of products/services. Products/services that are close to what the company offers in other markets would be a lower level of diversification than those that are radically different. Another orientation on diversification is determined by the degree of difference the new markets present from current markets. Similar languages and cultures would be a lower level of diversification than those that are different languages/cultures. The organizational capability and structure changes are often significant and are therefore difficult to summarize succinctly in a few bullet points. Capability strategies are further complicated by make/buy decisions. Deciding to build internally has vastly different capability requirements than establishing joint ventures or partnerships.

The opposite is also true: business contraction is a common cause for organizational redesign. Unfortunately, many reductions in force are performed without a formal review of organizational capabilities. Even when there are organizational design engagements as part of reductions, it is rare that a leadership team is even open to a discussion on capability trade-off's. Often times the leadership will make all-too-familiar requirements such as doing more with less and ensuring that we meet all our customers, stakeholder, and shareholder expectations but with a lower cost basis. The fallacy with this approach is apparent and obvious and can be best summed up with the following:

'All organizations are perfectly designed to get the results they get.'

Source unknown. Often attributed to W. Edwards Deming, Dr. Paul Batalden, or Donald Berwick.

What this means, as a base for organizational design, is that organizations are ecosystems. Change one thing and you impact everything else. Removing a percentage of the workforce (or a percentage of workforce costs) impacts organizational capabilities, even if the impact is "simply" capacity and throughput versus wholesale competence removal. Such contractions should be done planfully and strategically.

Business contractions with identified and defined strategic shifts are easier to address from an organizational standpoint than those where the strategic shifts remain undefined. While common, delegation of a reduction target to all departments is sub-optimal. Think about it for a moment: the opposite doesn't happen in a period of growth. Budget growth targets are never doled-out across departments with the message, 'every department can grow their costs by xx% this next year.' Growth is done with strategic guidance from leadership and growth targets set deliberately. A deliberate approach ensures the best use of the company's capital, and it intentionally drives the development of organizational capabilities. Equal, *if not greater*, care should be given to contraction. The loss of organizational capability impacts the company's products, services, value proposition, and people. After all, contraction-changes negatively impact people's lives and have substantial negative impact to a company's culture.

Simplicity Drives Adoption

The best organizational structure/design is not always the one that is the best from a design *architecture* standpoint. Employees must be able to understand the structure enough that they can see their roles, exercise their duties effectively, and believe in the direction of the organization. Acceptance and adoption are very powerful. It's similar in a sense to strategy. A company can have the best strategy in the world, but if the organization is not capable of executing on it, then it's not such a good strategy after all: because it results in failure. If the new organizational structure "checks all the boxes" and solves all the issues, but it's complex and convoluted, people will not accept it and it will fail. It may be better to make an incremental change in structure and to phase the remaining changes over time. Phasing the changes allows people the opportunity to learn about the capability needs and to put in place the decision rights, processes, systems, tools, talent, and incentives at a pace that is manageable. Phasing can help avoid over-taxation and ensure adoption.

Summary

The importance of being business-minded cannot be overstated. Practitioners in the organizational design space work on the business system itself. It is imperative that market value and differentiation be understood and that the practitioner is capable of interpreting business changes and how they may impact organizational structure. Establishing such a basis provides a good foundation from which to build. Each growth strategy warrants a formal review of organizational capability and structure. The degree of scaling and growth will determine the degree of formality that's needed in organizational design. As described in the previous chapter, compounded growth over time does merit formal reviews. It is also important to note that when a business contracts/shrinks, it is also vitally important to take an ecosystem and multidisciplinary view. Running quickly with "across the board" reduction targets risks unintended organizational capability losses.

Foundational Organizational Design Process

Chapter Focus

This chapter provides a summary of a foundational organizational design process. It is process oriented in that it provides the sequencing of steps and a review of the content of each step. References are cited for additional reading and development of foundational organizational design skills.

This chapter provides a *summary* of a foundational organizational design process. External resources are provided for those who wish to explore the foundations of organizational design further. The process of an organizational design engagement is described, so that the discrete steps can be built upon in the rest of the book. This chapter provides the basis for placing the organizational design discipline within context of the other six disciplines that will be explored in-depth in the subsequent chapters. The content of this chapter is intended to be a synopsis of the organizational design process. See Burton, Obel, & Hakonsson (2015) and Galbraith (1995) for additional knowledge and skill development in organizational design.

A couple quick internet searches and you will discover that there are quite a few resources on organizational design. Much of what is available focuses on organizational design and change management, where change management is positioned as the quintessential paired discipline. It is essential for a practitioner to have a thorough depth of understanding, and extensive experience base, in both organizational design and change management. These are foundations, and establishing a good foundation is essential. If you study one of the college-level textbooks on organizational design, it won't feel foundational. There's a lot to learn, even to conduct basic organizational design engagements such as one department or a small functional area. As is evidenced by the reported failure rates of organizational change initiatives, it is far more common to be dealing with complex performance issues where simple organizational design approaches are frankly insufficient. When the organizational redesigns are more complex, expertise is needed across disciplines. Cross-discipline expertise allows the business to identify, define, and derive the needed *capability* changes that deliver performance improvement. Consequently, it becomes important to know when to use internal resources that have foundational knowledge versus external specialists that have advanced knowledge, tools, research, and extensive experience across disciplines.

A good parallel comparison is auto repair. Trained mechanics share foundational knowledge about automobiles; they know the basics of the systems of automobiles (e.g. fuel, electrical, mechanical.) If you need to take your vehicle in for items like tires, lights, oil changes, filter changes, windshield wipers, and even brakes, your options for service providers are broad. If the issues are more complicated, you will receive better service from a specialist. If you're having performance issues with the engine, and it doesn't have the acceleration it should and there's a vibration, you are probably best to take your vehicle to a dealer. A dealer's mechanics are trained on advanced diagnostics and tools on your specific make/model of vehicle. You can take a gamble at a generic shop, but it is just that…a gamble. The former will have the resources, knowledge, and experience to diagnose the problem and repair/replace the needed components to correct the performance issue. The latter spend most of their time doing oil changes, tires, brakes, and general maintenance, and they may be unable to sufficiently diagnose the problem. There are always generic shops that will try to diagnose and fix your vehicle anyway, and they inevitably end up performing what's called Field Replaceable Unit (FRU) procedures where they remove and replace components *likely* to cause the problem. They'll do this until the problem corrects itself. On an automobile repair, this results in a larger-than-needed list of new parts that cost more money.

Similarly, in organizational design, if you are doing some simple scaling-up and adding a manager and a few direct reports, a generalist is certainly capable of facilitating the engagement. If instead, your company is struggling with performance that spans functions, departments, and geographies, having a multi-disciplinary specialist is the better choice. Applying a generalist to complex organizational performance issues often results in more and more people being impacted by structure changes, when the performance issues are caused by multiple items that need to be addressed together.

Participation

Before looking at the organizational design process, a first premise is that of *participation*. Through experience, there is a tendency for leadership to make organizational design engagements "confidential." There are situations where a high degree of confidentiality is essential, such as governance changes, mergers, acquisitions, and other similar changes where the knowledge of the change would risk the strategy itself. However, that's a small percentage of the organizational design engagements that occur within a company. Most organizational design engagements deal with business performance issues, and to fully solve for performance issues, a team approach is necessary. *Participation* is a key to success in an organizational design engagement; a variety of people/backgrounds are needed for accurate and thorough inputs all the way through the process. The larger and more complex the company, the more important it is to take a team approach.

There's a concept in organizational research called *information asymmetry*. Information asymmetry means that there is a knowledge gap between every manager and their employee. The act of delegating tasks, by its very nature, means that an employee will have a fuller knowledge of those tasks because of their close proximity to them. Therefore, the employee possesses knowledge that the manager does not; the knowledge gap is unavoidable. The larger the organization, the more layers, the more dispersion, the more difficult it becomes for a manager to have a thorough knowledgebase of the work and how it is performed. It becomes exponentially more difficult to have the knowledge necessary to successfully design effective organizational solutions. Effective solutions must simultaneously deliver the needed *improvements* while *preserving* current organizational capabilities. The balance of making *improvements* while *preserving capabilities* is the cornerstone of the need for a team approach. For this reason, engagements conducted in isolation are usually not recommended (barring strategic and intellectual property constraints mentioned earlier.) Instead, it is recommended to be deliberate about team selection to ensure breadth and depth of knowledge and expertise. Along with the selected team, the deciding leader should be involved in the process from beginning to end.

The selection of the team is dependent upon at least the following anticipated changes: business performance, product/service strategy, value proposition, and organizational capabilities. From these, the areas of the organization expected to be impacted can be identified and also represented on the team. Organization design is more than a human resources project or an act of high-level governance. All aspects of a company's performance and ability to function are at stake. The positive implication of doing a great job is future success and growth. The negative implication of doing a poor job is future failure and shrinkage, which may also generate an organizational redesign cycle that erodes culture and trust. Having the right participation up front and throughout the engagement helps ensure a holistic view of what needs to change and what needs to be preserved.

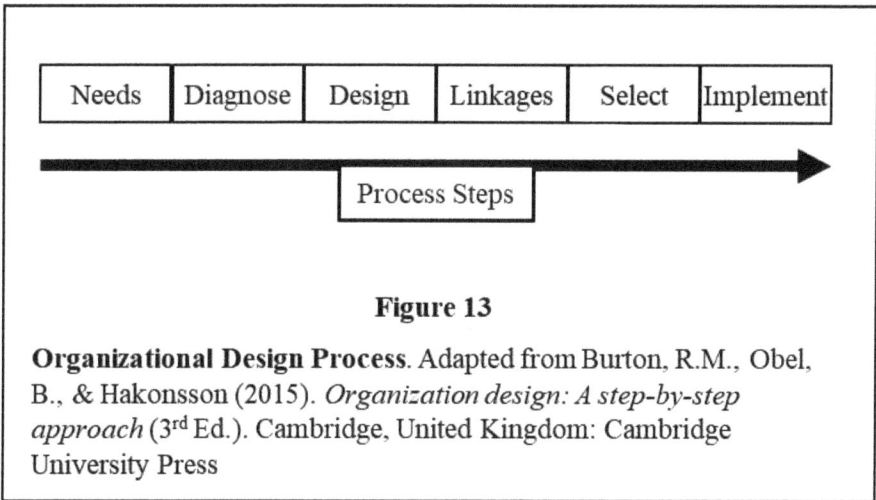

Needs	Diagnose	Design	Linkages	Select	Implement

Process Steps

Figure 13

Organizational Design Process. Adapted from Burton, R.M., Obel, B., & Hakonsson (2015). *Organization design: A step-by-step approach* (3rd Ed.). Cambridge, United Kingdom: Cambridge University Press

Organizational Design Process

The process presented in this section has broad application across many types of organizations. As stated earlier, reviewing the organizational design process allows further development of the multi-disciplinary approach to organizational design; this does not replace in-depth training and experience in the discipline of organizational design itself. Experience means a lot in this area of practice.

A basic organization design process consists of six steps, as shown in Figure 13. This process can be used in an organizational design engagement at any level in a business. It is also common in very large companies to have multiple design projects active simultaneously. In this case it is recommended that all organizational design engagements be connected as each one will impact the business ecosystem. Each step of the process with be briefly explained.

Needs: The aim of this step is to develop a set of *business needs* that must be achieved. Engagements usually start with a request from a manager along with that person's perspective on the problem, cause, and solution. Most managers will engage with what they believe the solution should be, at least in-part. It is important to understand that this is an initial presentation, and while you might get lucky and find a manager who has fully vetted the business needs, this is usually not the case. Issues are often expressed in terms of inefficiencies, ineffectiveness, and unhealthy conflict. Listen to the presented issues and work through a series of probing questions that trace the symptoms back to a *business need.*

Take for example an outside sales force where one of the expressed issues was a problem with unequal territory sizes between sales agents and their sales managers. The manager wanted to balance the territory sizes to drive fairness and equity along with improving the efficiencies of the team. This was reasonable, and it was a valid perspective. A dialogue, along with some probing questions went like this:

Practitioner: What efficiency gains do you believe a realignment would provide?

Manager: Our agents spend unequal amounts of time with their customers because of the differences in loading. Realigning would allow us to equalize the time spent with customers.

Practitioner: Why is spending equal amounts of time with each customer important?

Manager: It helps us ensure a consistent quality of interaction and service.

Practitioner: What sort of a result does that provide to the business?

Manager: Well several things, but the biggest one is that it promotes *customer retention.*

Practitioner: So, would you say that *customer retention* is a business need that you would like to see improved as part of this effort?

Manager: Absolutely.

In this example, *customer retention* became a *business need*, which was then used in a list of criteria to assess alternative organization designs. Needs are derived through discussions and interviews that proceed much like the above sample dialogue. Sometimes it is useful to use other qualitative methods such as focus groups and observations. A list of business needs is subsequently used as design criteria to evaluate the projected impact of organizational changes.

Diagnose: The aim of this step is to determine the root cause(s) of the performance gaps. This builds on the previous step where the business needs were identified. When approaching the performance issues from a purely organizational design perspective, the aim of this step is to determine *if* the organizational structure is contributing to the gap and *if* changes would help correct the performance. Quantitative methods, including relevant data research and analysis is recommended where available.

Note: There are significant differences between a classic organizational design process and *organizational design that sticks.* One of those differences is in the approach to diagnostics. This will be described in detail in subsequent chapters.

When the diagnosis reveals strategic adjustments, political/power shifts, business growth/shrinkage, or leadership changes, organizational redesign may be necessary to bridge performance gaps. Strategic adjustments and business growth/shrinkage are strong signals that there are *capability* changes needed. Political/power shifts, and leadership changes may or may not indicate capability changes, but they should herald extreme caution to ensure that any organizational redesigns do not compromise organizational capability, value proposition, or product/service mix. Additional causes of performance gaps can include unhealthy conflict, ineffective workflow, internal or external responsiveness issues, role confusion, ineffective resource application (people, capex, or opex), and presence of duplicative organizations. These may warrant an organizational redesign. Wherever there are performance gaps, the team must make a determination whether organizational changes will address and correct the performance.

Design: If the preceding steps indicate that organizational structure is one of the contributing factors to the performance gap, the engagement can continue into the design step. In this step, the business needs are brought forward and are used as design criteria. The team works through a brainstorming and exploration process where they consider alternative organizational structures. There are five organizing themes that can be explored: functional, geographic, product/service, customer segment, and process. Where advantageous, these can be blended to create combinations within an organization level. They can also be combined to create matrixed and hybrid structures.

The design step is best performed as a working team, with a facilitator, and often in a workshop environment. An excellent way to conduct the workshop is to go through the following:

1) Start with a strategy presentation on the business. This helps to ground the team in current business performance and future direction.

2) Review the business needs that were identified in the "needs" step, and ensure that they align with the company's view of the future.

3) Brief the team on the outcome of the "diagnosis" step, and call-out those root causes where organizational structure may help to address performance gaps.

4) Have each team member present their current organizational structure along with their view of an analysis on that structure. A Strengths, Weaknesses, Opportunities, and Threats (SWOT) analysis is a good tool to use. Each team member can prepare their SWOT analysis in advance of the workshop. If desired, this is a good opportunity to collect broader input from within the organization. The strengths and weaknesses assessment will provide good internal context, and the opportunities and threats assessment will provide good external context.

5) Present the team with information on the organizational themes available for consideration, along with the strengths and weaknesses of each theme. Additionally, information can be provided around the company's higher-level structure and governance process.

6) Facilitate brainstorming on organizational alternatives. The richest ideation will flow from an open brainstorming technique where all ideas are solicited without critique or discussion at this step.

7) Work through assembling, modifying, and adjusting the ideas into new structural alternatives. As variations arise, capture those as additional alternatives.

To generate additional ideation, benchmarking can also be done. Benchmarking can be as simple as collecting available data or as complicated as formal benchmarking tours with identified companies. If benchmarking is conducted, it is important to ground the team in the interdependent organizational constructs (IOCs) shown in Figure 11. Inevitably, all companies have a different mix of products/services, value disciplines, and organizational capabilities. While benchmarking is a fantastic way to stimulate thinking, it could be detrimental to adopt another company's organizational structure in whole or in part. The intent should not be to use another company's structure, but instead to breakaway from "normal thinking," and to offer the team a real-life case study of how others approach markets differently.

Once the design work is completed, the team should graphically depict the alternative(s). It is recommended that multiple alternatives be generated, so that the variations on organizational themes can be explained and evaluated.

Linkages: Every organizational structure has its own set of strengths and weaknesses; consequently, every structure depends on linkages to make it work. These links include processes, systems, incentives, and talent to name a few. It is beneficial to address the linkages in the same workshop as the design. The design workshop will generate a lot of fresh thinking and ideas, and in the formulation of organizational alternatives it is natural to talk through the other linkages that will be required. Applying another SWOT analysis to the organizational design alternatives can help derive linkages, especially focusing on the internal weaknesses. It's the internal weaknesses that need to be mitigated to enable the new organizational structure. Identify linkages for each alternative generated in the previous step, so a full picture of the scope of work can be developed and presented. Wherever the organizational design alternatives impact the IOC's, shown in Figure 11, these impacts need to be fully developed. Any impacts to product/services, value disciplines, and organizational capabilities will have a bearing on the company's market position and market value.

Select: In this step, the working team decides which organizational structure is the best choice to bridge the performance gap(s). The team should evaluate each organizational alternative against the design criteria that was developed in the "needs" and "design" steps. Establishing a scale and scoring each alternative is useful, as it provides a level of rating and adds some additional objectivity to the process. There are many different approaches that can be used for rating scales; a professional organizational design facilitator will have a toolkit that can be used for this and every other step of the process. The goal is to assess, evaluate, and select the best organizational alternative.

Often the working team makes a recommendation up to a *decider*. When presenting, the working team should provide a synopsis of the process, all previous work, and the evaluation/scoring. The team should also ensure that the decider is aware of the linkages that are needed for successful implementation of the recommended structure. There are costs/investments required for any change, and it will be necessary to take those into account prior to rendering a decision.

Implement: Implementation is the last step in the organizational design process. It is critical to do a *great* job with implementation. The best organizational design can be ruined with poor implementation. Conversely, a mediocre organizational design can be a remarkable success if the implementation is handled with excellence. The working team is in the best position to see the organizational changes through implementation; they have all of the context. Insights have been generated throughout the process, and that information can be leveraged to ensure a successful implementation.

Summary

This was a short synopsis of a fundamental organizational design process. It was intended as an overview to refresh the reader. The following chapters build upon this knowledge base. This chapter was not intended to replace deep skill development in the body of knowledge of organizational design. You are encouraged to use available resources to further develop as needed, including the references provided here and available learning and development programs from leading institutions.

Organizational Design That Sticks

Chapter Focus

To achieve organizational designs *that stick*, it's necessary to employ a multi-disciplinary approach to solving business problems. Improving firm-level performance requires working on the ecosystem itself.

From the earlier chapter on "A Persistent Business Problem," it's clear that a new and revised approach to organizational design is long overdue. Having an estimated 1.5 billion people worldwide experiencing organizational redesign failures every year is unacceptable.

Applying a multi-disciplinary approach solves for the execution gap. This is not a new recommendation; business advisors and scholars have been writing about this approach for decades. For example, one of the flagship publications on organizational design was written by Ernest Dale in 1967, and published by the American Management Association. He outlines an approach that incorporates structure, decision rights, and company economics. He even cited sources going back decades earlier. Another example, represented by one of the most famous historical organizational charts in modern history, was developed for the New York and Eerie Railroads, shown in Figure 14 (McCallum & Henshaw, 1855). This chart has a very organic and natural form, looking more like a tree versus our modern pyramid-like charts. When developed, the chart's purpose was to depict multiple disciplines: flow of information and data, decision rights and authority

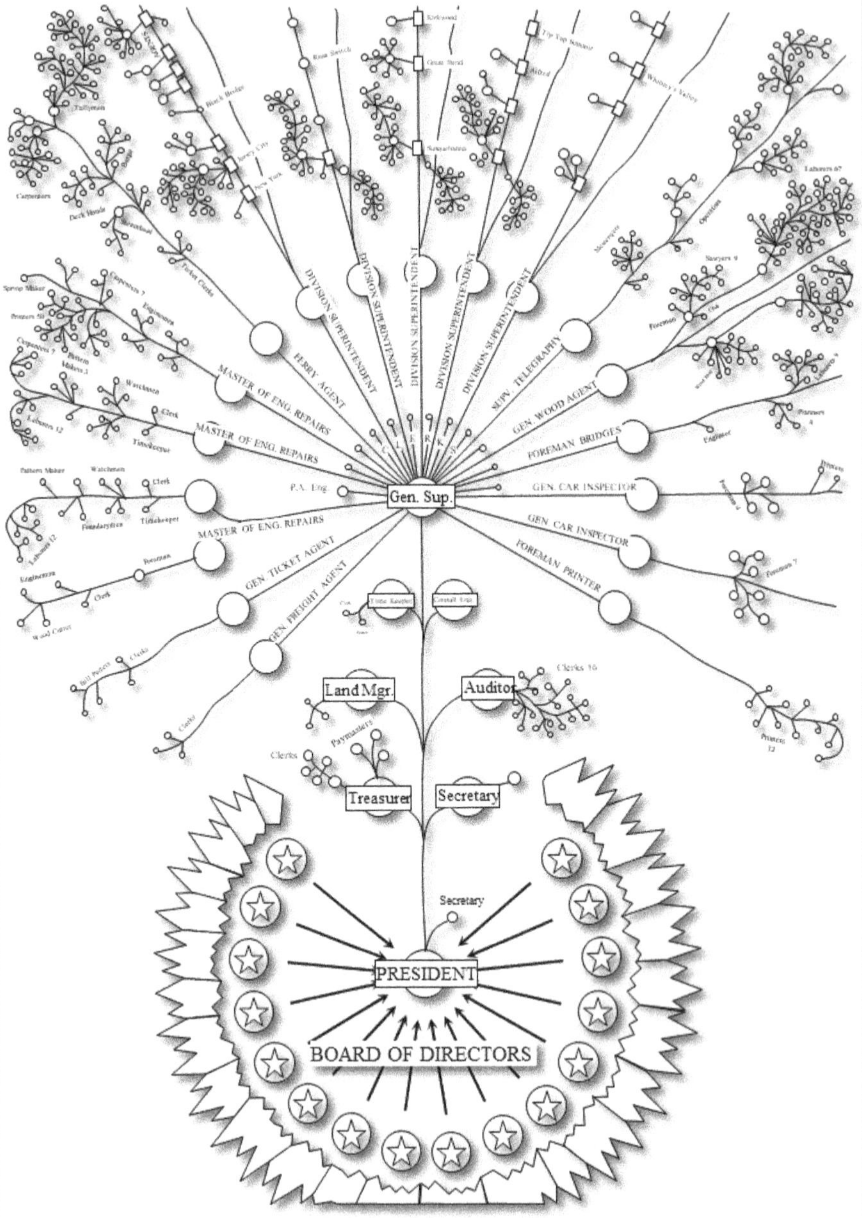

Figure 14

Organizational Chart for the New York and Erie Railroad: Adapted from (redrawn) McCallum & Henshaw (1855). [Public Domain].

levels, geographical dispersion, structure, and number of employees. It is evidence of a multi-disciplinary/holistic approach to the company as an ecosystem.

Organizational charting itself goes back thousands of years. Ancient civilizations, when they charted, most commonly charted the structures of their governments, territories, and military. As an example, the Egyptian cartouche is a vertically oriented set of hieroglyphs depicting the names and titles of a structure of authority, hierarchy, and importance, with the names and titles of the most important at the top.

The multi-disciplinary and ecosystem approach contrasts with the modern reductionist approach that's common in western cultures. Reductionism takes something that is whole and complex, and breaks it down into parts. The aim being to reduce the complex into more fundamental and basic elements that can be better understood and subsequently solved. *Not to be misinterpreted, reductionism has served us well!* The industrial age was in large-part enabled by reductionism. The advent of the assembly line, most often attributed to Henry Ford, was (and is) a pinnacle example of reductionism: breaking down the complexity of an automobile into a series of smaller tasks and more fundamental assemblage of parts. When performed, job and task analyses are exercises in reductionism, resulting in job descriptions that represent the division of labor within a company. They are an application of reductionism. The organizational chart itself codifies the company's view of the division of labor, distribution of tasks and authorities, and how it sees its work in a reduced view. Conducting a "pure" organizational design engagement is a reductionist endeavor because, at its core, it is the division of labor into parent/child relationships.

Deriving an effective and efficient division of labor will always be a core need, but doing so while positively impacting the performance outcome of the whole business, in a desired way, gives the design

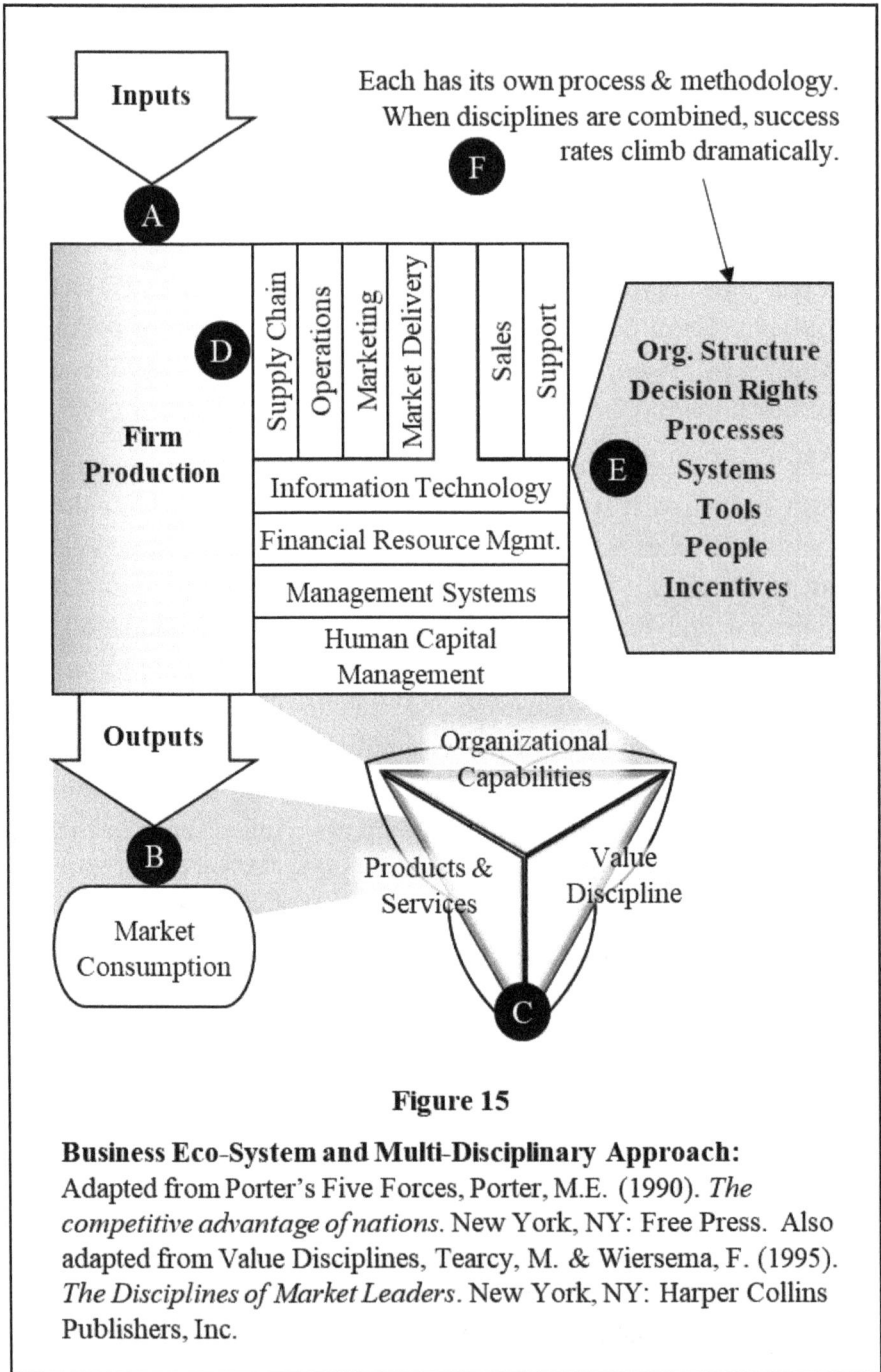

Inputs

Each has its own process & methodology. When disciplines are combined, success rates climb dramatically.

F

A

D

Supply Chain | Operations | Marketing | Market Delivery | Sales | Support

Firm Production

Information Technology

Financial Resource Mgmt.

Management Systems

Human Capital Management

E

Org. Structure
Decision Rights
Processes
Systems
Tools
People
Incentives

Outputs

B

Market Consumption

Organizational Capabilities

Products & Services

Value Discipline

C

Figure 15

Business Eco-System and Multi-Disciplinary Approach:
Adapted from Porter's Five Forces, Porter, M.E. (1990). *The competitive advantage of nations*. New York, NY: Free Press. Also adapted from Value Disciplines, Tearcy, M. & Wiersema, F. (1995). *The Disciplines of Market Leaders*. New York, NY: Harper Collins Publishers, Inc.

sticking-power. To do so, the business must be viewed as an ecosystem, and organizational design must be approached in a multidisciplinary manner. Figure 15 depicts a model and macro-level process for organizational design engagements *that stick*. The rest of this chapter will refer to Figure 15 and work through a thorough explanation of the model.

The vertical flow at the left of Figure 15 (A) is intended to characterize all types of companies: for-profit, non-profit, commercial, and governmental. All companies take inputs, shape and exercise those inputs, and form outputs. Those outputs are subsequently consumed in a marketplace (B). This is a simple way to frame and define value chains. To map a value chain, one only needs to repeat this sequence of *inputs*, *production*, and *outputs* for each company that forms a node in the value chain.

For example, a simple map of the value chain of an application development company is shown in Figure 16. Jim's Application Company produces "app's" (A) that are sold in two digital marketplaces (B). Each marketplace is based on a different device operating system, shown as a pear and a robot. The production activity of Jim's Application Company is primarily coding (C). The people employed there take the inputs and apply their own knowledge, skill, and labor to code new applications. A few of the inputs (D) that the company relies on include computers, programming languages, communications systems, and software development kits (SDK's). The company procures these from other suppliers and uses them in its own production processes.

To extend this upstream into the supply chain, the same mapping technique can be employed. While the use of computers is an input to Jim's Application Company, those same computers are someone else's output (E). Figure 16 shows two instances of going up in the value chain with the map. The primary production activity of the company that produces computers (i.e. servers, PC's, and laptops) as their output

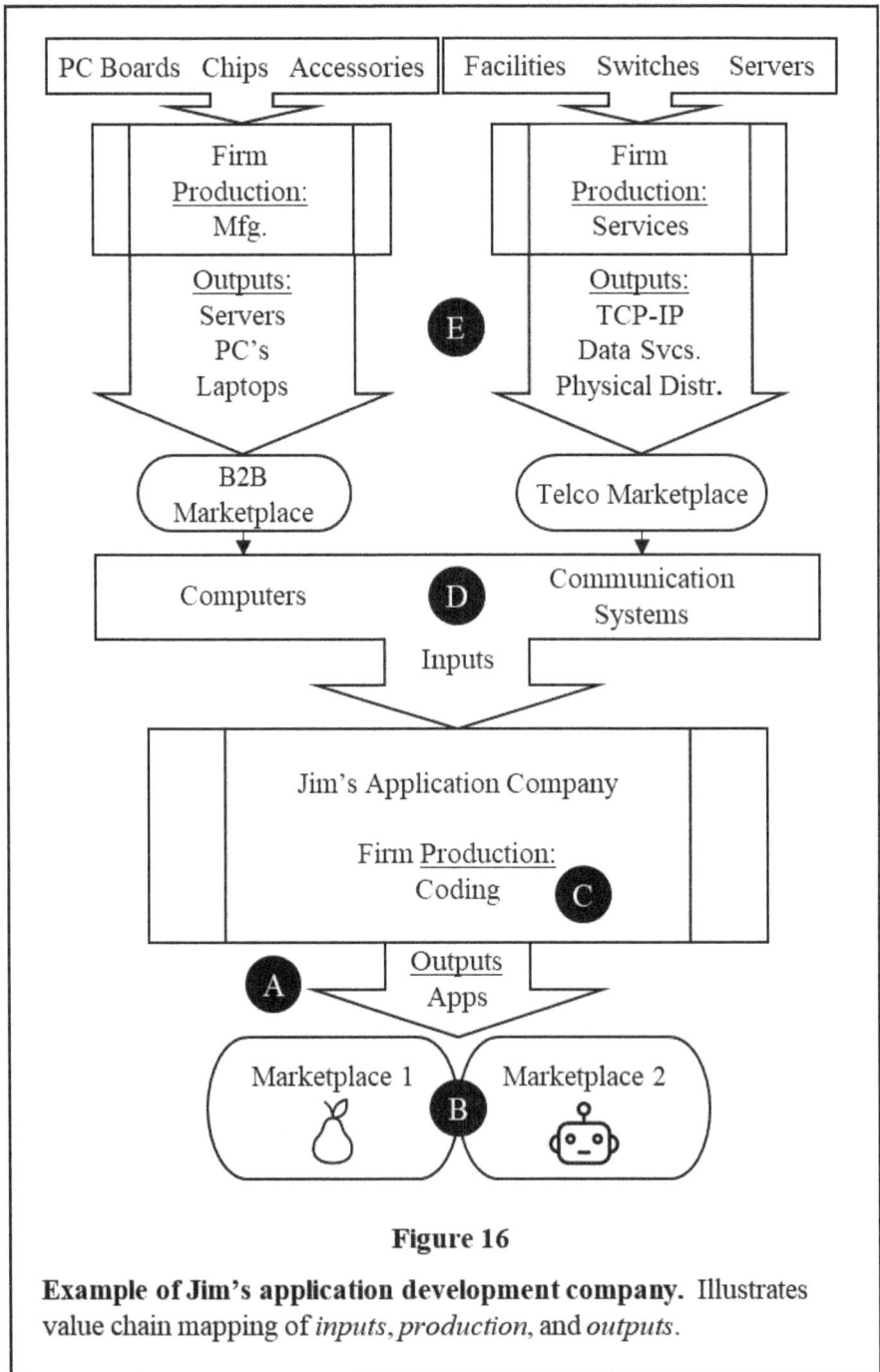

Figure 16

Example of Jim's application development company. Illustrates value chain mapping of *inputs, production,* and *outputs.*

is manufacturing. For their inputs they procure PC boards, chips, and accessories. The communications system, that Jim's Application Company relies on as an input, comes from a telecommunications company. They provide, as their outputs, TCP-IP and data services (commonly referred to as the internet) over a physical network. The primary production activities are services. As some of their inputs, they rely on facilities, telecom switches, and servers. This simple diagram shows only two inputs, but the diagramming of inputs, company production, and outputs (Figure 15-A) can be repeated until a full picture of a company's value chain is produced both upstream and downstream. The outputs move into a marketplace (Figure 15-B) for consumption, and what is delivered is a reflection of the company's choices around the interdependent organizational constructs (IOC's) (Figure 15-C and previously in Figure 11.) The company chooses to deliver a certain mix of product/service, customer intimacy, and operational excellence. The choices that are made by the company, related to IOCs, directly impact the *organizational capabilities* that are needed (Figure 15-C.) The organization is built to deliver a certain mix of products, services, and value disciplines.

A commonly used model for viewing supply chain functions, which is also useful for framing organizational capabilities, is shown in Figure 15-D. This might be familiar to you, as it is adopted from Porter's (1998) value-chain work. The model shown has been modified to fit the realities of the early 21st century. Each block represents a type/category of work that needs to be performed, and each label is what's commonly seen in most companies. Using a framework like this is the first layer of reductionism, breaking down the productive value of the company into sub-components. The categories of work along the top represent work that *directly* touches the products/services as either inputs, production, or outputs. The categories of work along the bottom represent work that *indirectly* affects the products/services, often seen as support functions. Information technology (IT) has been uniquely depicted as being capable of existing in either a *direct* or *indirect* capacity. The nature of the company's products/services will determine whether IT is a direct or indirect function. The example in Figure 16, for Jim's Application Company, IT services can be viewed as a *direct* function because the application design and development *is* the product.

The *direct* types/categories of work include supply chain, operations, marketing, market delivery, information technology, sales, and support. Each will be briefly described.

- Supply chain acquires the needed inputs for the company, typically through activities such as sourcing, procurement, inventory planning/management, and merchandising.

- Operations does the conversion work from inputs to new outputs, typically through activities such as development, manufacturing, assembly, and integration.

- Marketing generates market awareness and customer traffic through branding, advertising, and price management.

- Market delivery concerns itself with placing products/services in the marketplace. In Porter's (1998) model, this was called logistics; however, since digital markets have become prevalent, the term "logistics" is not the best choice as it implies the physical movement of goods. "Market delivery" is more generic and can be applied to the placement of products/services in either a virtual or physical marketplace.

- Information technology, as a direct category of work, concerns itself with the IT aspects of producing products/services for market consumption, and it includes things like development operations, product lifecycle management, quality assurance, and product hosting.

- Sales converts customer traffic into contracts or purchases through either direct or indirect sales (outside or inside), and it includes other activities such as account management, territory management, and account planning.

- Support ensures market and customer adoption and satisfaction through activities related to installation, troubleshooting, maintenance, and customer knowledge and skill development.

The *indirect* types/categories of work include information technology, financial resource management, management systems, and human capital management.

- Information technology as an *indirect* category of work addresses the support requirements of the company, and it includes activities such as computing platforms, application specification and builds, hardware and software deployment, information storage and processing, and desktop support.

- Financial resource management processes, sorts, and reports on the company's monies, and this includes activities such as treasury, taxation, accounting, securities, and payroll.

- Management systems is the "glue" for the business and ensures that a company has a cadence and method that's understood and followed, and it includes activities such as strategy, business reviews, project/program management, scorecarding, data sciences, and business intelligence.

- Human capital management has everything to do with people and includes activities such as talent acquisition, talent development, culture, rewards, benefits, facilities, and policy management.

The *direct* and *indirect* types/categories of activities all work together to deliver a set of organizational capabilities, which in-turn delivers a mix of product/service and value disciplines to the market. Inputs (Figure 15-A) come into the company, and the ten categories of activities (Figure 15-D) shape and exercise them to form outputs to be consumed in the marketplace (Figure 15-B.) All companies of all types do some form of conversion activity. A company's macro-level effectiveness can be measured by how well they deliver their products/services compared to their competition and compared to other substitutes. A company's efficiency can be measured by the amount of resources it uses to convert inputs into outputs.

When a company consciously and deliberately defines the organizational capabilities needed, improvements in effectiveness and efficiency come through a set of seven disciplines (Figure 15-E.)

The seven disciplines that need to be exercised include:

1. Organizational Structure
2. Decision Rights
3. Process Design
4. Systems
5. Tools
6. People
7. Incentives

Other works have been published that express three, four, and five disciplines. Limiting the disciplines might make some things easier, but it also predisposes one to miss key work activities that are essential for driving change. There are *at least* seven disciplines that need to be exercised, and all seven are amazingly important to driving improvement changes. Using other methods that limit these inevitably results in underachievement of the performance improvement needed in the business ecosystem. Each discipline (Figure 15-F) has its own methodology that needs to be understood in order to use them together to drive desired changes. The body of knowledge in each is substantial; consequently, each should be given its fair consideration.

Organizational structure was addressed in the previous chapter on "foundational organizational design process." There's a reason that it's common for new leaders to address organizational structure first. Human beings are inherently social, and structuring our social interactions comes naturally to us. One only need to watch kids on a playground to learn this fundamental human truth. Children naturally organize themselves into groups with hierarchies, and this natural inclination continues throughout our lives. Company structure both expresses and implies much about methods of operation, authorities, culture, and market orientation. Firm structure also expresses and implies much about the people who construct it.

Once completed, an organizational design expresses a formal relationship of the division of labor. The organizational structure is often the formal expression of the *desired* organizational capabilities (Figure 15-D.) New organizational designs are *aspirational*; they are an expression of what is *desired*. The first step in implementation is usually moving the reporting relationships around; however, making a new organizational design *real* depends on many/all of the remaining disciplines (Figure 15-E.) Making the new organizational design real means to *operate the business* as defined. Operationalizing the organization is always more than boxes and lines on a chart. It depends on decision rights, processes, systems, tools, people, and incentives, all working together to function as desired.

Decision rights formalize the informal. Organizational design practitioners have long pined about the difference between the formal organizational structure and the informal power structure. The informal power structure controls decisions and resources. The discipline of decision rights is about expressly bringing forward the key decisions and making their operation a matter of deliberation and discussion, with the goal being to do what's optimal for the business.

In any given company, there are hundreds and thousands of decisions made on a daily basis. Trying to address them all would land one inside a personal experience in the law of diminishing returns. It is most beneficial to focus on *key* decisions. Key decisions address strategic and critical resources such as:

- Capital Expenditures (CAPEX)

- Operational Expenditures (OPEX)
- People allocations (both people and time)
- Physical resource utilization (equipment and facilities)

These four decision themes govern decision matrices, and all four of these types of decisions have cascading implications. Take for example the decisions around capital investments and expenditures. The CEO makes a recommendation to the board regarding investment level, and the board approves. The CEO then distributes capital allocations to each of the business segments. The leader of each business segment distributes capital to departments, initiatives, and projects. Within each department, initiative, and project there are further allocations to specific work. Cascading happens at increasing levels of detail. There is also a counter-balancing mechanism. CEO's don't walk into board meetings and just guess at what's needed for capital expenditures. The recommendation mechanism is a series of aggregations that come up through the organization. The same aggregation and cascading mechanism operates for all four themes: CAPEX, OPEX, people allocations, and physical resource allocations.

Identifying the key decisions, defining who owns them at each level, and then communicating that to the organization, drives decision effectiveness. Clarity on decision rights and ownership is paramount. Without clarity, an organization will struggle to improve both decision quality and speed. Without clarity of ownership it is difficult to drive accountability for the content and direction of decisions. Without clarity of ownership, people will struggle to move decisions to the right place in the organization, slowing down the entire ecosystem.

There are those that will react to this in a negative manner and think that this is too bureaucratic of an effort, and that it will slow down the organization. However, leaving decision rights unaddressed means that there's a belief that the organization will operate more effectively if the decision rights are implied versus defined. Leaving decision rights implied means that leadership believes that things will get figured out naturally; the reality is that the new and needed changes in decision rights never really move anywhere. Implied decision rights leave significant groups of people uninformed and eventually leads to poor clarity, quality, and speed of decision making.

Processes both govern and reflect the work that's performed in the conversion of inputs into outputs (Figure 15-A.) Additionally, they illustrate how work moves between and within each of the core and supporting functions in the value chain (Figure 15-D.) Processes are a critical discipline for impacting the performance of the ecosystem, because well-fitted processes optimize resource utilization. Poorly fitted processes waste organizational resources. It's as simple as that.

Process discipline is essential to performance, but it comes with a caveat: *processes are made for the organization, the organization is not made for processes.* In other words, there is always a right level of detail and rigor in process design. Too little and the organization will struggle with consistency in execution, putting at-risk the ability to produce quality and timely outputs. Too much process rigor and the organization will struggle with sluggish execution, embodied in endless forms, checklists, and multiple levels of approvals and sign-off's. Every organization needs to pay particular attention to ensuring proper *process fitment.*

A process, in its simplest definition, is a depiction of how a set of tasks are performed to derive an output. Properly fitted processes reflect and direct the use of the company's resources, and they codify organizational capabilities. For example, consider the same output from two different companies with different processes: sneakers. For illustration simplicity, both companies produce exactly the same sneaker design, and they go to market through an on-line ordering process along with direct shipping to their customers. They have, however, implemented different *processes.* Those process differences give them each a unique set of organizational capabilities, and they also give them a different value proposition in the marketplace. All based on a few differences in the process.

At Josephina's Sneaker Company, Figure 17, they have decided to implement a cellular manufacturing process. Each process step inside the manufacturing circle is a person, and they create each sneaker as an order comes in from a customer. Because each order is made to a set of customer requests, this is called a "make-to-order" process. The product variability that Josefina allows is color. Customers can choose material colors in the sole, insole, each piece of the uppers, and in the laces.

Referring to Figures 15 and 17; Josefina's company is:

- A & B: Taking raw materials and producing sneakers for market consumption.

- C: Producing a product – sneakers. The value discipline that differentiates them in the marketplace is the customer's ability to customize colors. This means that they need the organizational capability to manufacture in a make-to-order manner and produce a high-mix of product variability.

- D: This informs what each of the value chain functions must deliver in terms of organizational capability:

  o The *supply chain* capability needed is the ability to balance high mix with lead times. The supply chain must source the same materials but in a wide variety of colors. This will present a challenge with inventory, as stocking all the assorted colors could become costly, and shipping them in one at a time from suppliers would cause lead-time and coordination issues.

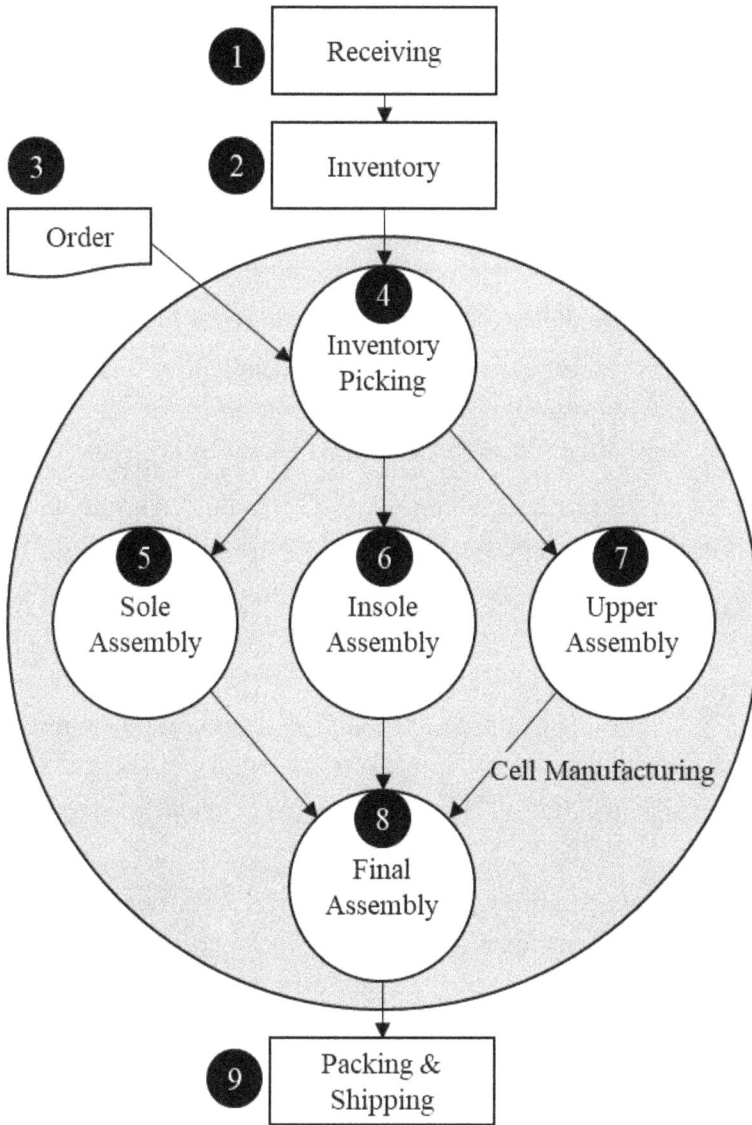

Figure 17

Josephina's Sneaker Company. Implementing a cell manufacturing process to produce products that are customized to each order.

- o The *operations* capability needed is the ability to produce products in a make-to-order manner. This necessitates a high skill/craft level in the manufacturing team, and the quality of the product will need to balance with the time to produce.

- o *Marketing* will need to be capable of reaching a customer base that values color customization. This informs customer segmentation, target markets, branding, and advertising approaches.

- o Market delivery requires the capability to ship directly to customers. This will inform the shipping partnerships and materials needed.

- o Information technology (IT), in this example, is a direct function, as it needs to provide the capability of an on-line marketplace for the customer. Given Josephina's value proposition of customization, IT needs to provide order customization.

- o In this example, sales and support could be combined to provide organizational capability of supporting customer ordering and follow-up via phone, email, and chat.

- o The indirect functions of IT, finance, human capital, and management systems would need to be designed to enable the above capabilities in an effective and efficient manner.

- E: The cellular manufacturing process allows for a high-degree of customization, and it contains 9 process steps (Figure 17):

  1. Receiving

  2. Inventory Materials

3. Order Processing

4. Inventory Picking

5. Assemble Sole

6. Assemble Insole

7. Assemble Uppers

8. Final Assembly

9. Packing & Shipping

Let's contrast this with Joseph's Sneaker Company, shown in Figure 18. Joseph has decided to implement a line-manufacturing process. Each process step inside the "line manufacturing" box is at least one person and can be scaled to meet volume requirements. They produce one sneaker design with no variability. Each sneaker is manufactured and then placed into finished goods inventory, and as an order comes in, the shipping department packs and ships it immediately. Because each sneaker is made in a standard manner and placed in inventory, this is called a "make-to-inventory" process. The market difference that Joseph's company provides is speed of delivery.

In contrast, Joseph does not allow product variability. Instead, he has built a process that ensures optimized speed and consistent product quality. Referring to Figures 15 and 18; Joseph's company is:

- A & B: Taking raw materials and producing sneakers for market consumption – same essential production as Josefina's company.

- C: Producing a product – sneakers. The value discipline that differentiates Joseph's company in the marketplace is speed and consistency in quality. This means that they need the organizational capability to manufacture in a manner that produces both volume and consistency.

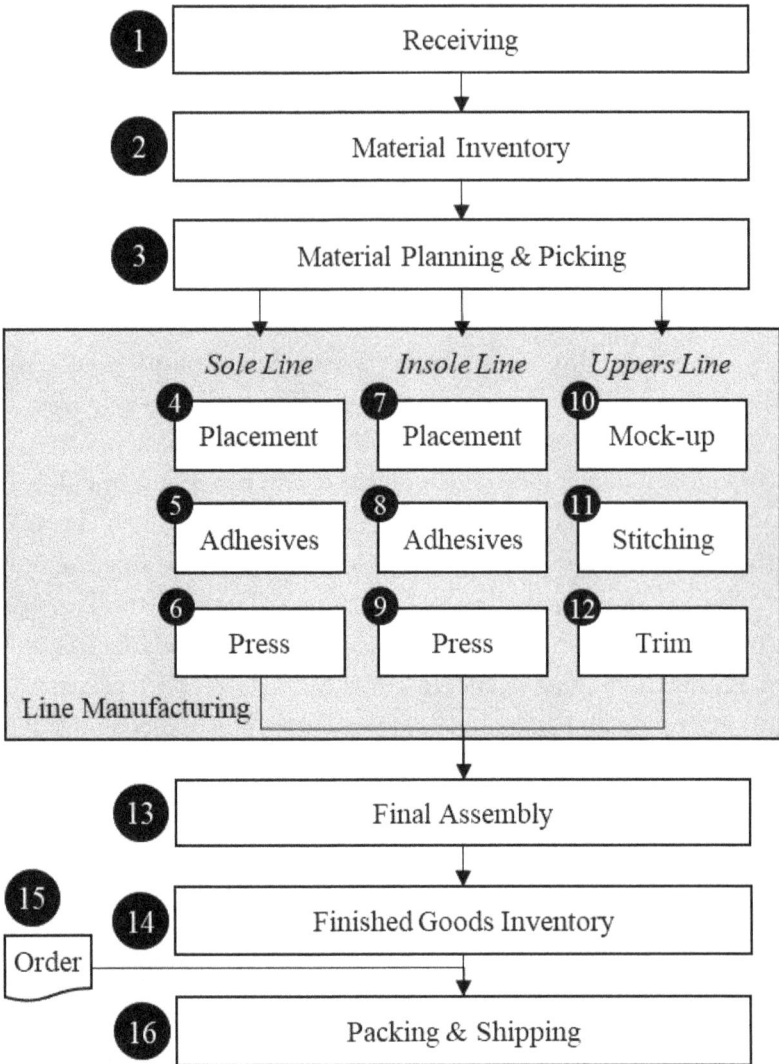

1 Receiving

2 Material Inventory

3 Material Planning & Picking

Sole Line   *Insole Line*   *Uppers Line*

4 Placement   **7** Placement   **10** Mock-up

5 Adhesives   **8** Adhesives   **11** Stitching

6 Press   **9** Press   **12** Trim

Line Manufacturing

13 Final Assembly

15 **14** Finished Goods Inventory

Order

16 Packing & Shipping

Figure 18

Joseph's Sneaker Company. Implementing a line manufacturing process to produce products faster and more consistently.

- D: This informs what each of the value chain functions must deliver in terms of organizational capability:

    o The *supply chain* capability needed is the ability to source, procure, and inventory a set of materials that ensures a predefined production volume. The challenge for Joseph's supply chain will be inventory management: setting the thresholds for each part so that they minimize expenditures while guaranteeing production throughput.

    o The *operations* capability needed is the ability to produce products in a make-to-inventory manner. This requires a capital investment in manufacturing equipment, along with consistent staffing and skills. The manufacturing process chosen needs to be designed and managed for specified production volume.

    o *Marketing* will need to reach those customers who value speed and consistency in the product. This informs customer segmentation, target markets, branding, and advertising approaches.

    o Market delivery requires the capability to ship directly to customers. This will inform the shipping partnerships and materials needed for packing.

    o Information technology (IT), in this example, may be an indirect function, depending how customer orders are processed and tracked.

    o In this example, sales and support could be combined to provide organizational capability of supporting customer ordering and follow-up via phone, email, and chat. Given the product difference (standard product without customization) between the two companies, it is likely that Joseph will need fewer resources in sales and support.

- o The indirect functions of IT, finance, human capital, and management systems would need to be designed to enable the above capabilities in an effective and efficient manner.

- E: The line manufacturing process enables volume and consistency, and it contains 16 process steps (Figure 18):

  1. Receiving
  2. Inventory Materials
  3. Material Planning & Picking

  Sole Line

  4. Placement
  5. Adhesives
  6. Press

  Insole Line

  7. Placement
  8. Adhesives
  9. Press

  Uppers Line

  10. Mock-up
  11. Stitching
  12. Trim
  13. Final Assembly
  14. Finished Goods Inventory
  15. Order Processing
  16. Packing & Shipping

The process difference between these two companies is significant. Even in these simple examples, with a high-level drawing, the results alter each of the systemic elements shown in Figure 15-C: organizational capabilities, value disciplines, and products. The process choice impacts the disciplines (Figure 15-E); it impacts organizational structure, decision rights, systems, tools, people, and incentives. One can easily argue that some of these other disciplines should be addressed prior to making process decisions, which further strengthens the point that our businesses operate as ecosystems and that each of these disciplines are interdependent.

There is one part of the indirect supply chain that warrants special mention: management systems (Figure 15-D.) Every business, no matter how small or large, needs a defined management system. It is justifiably the most important process for any business. Whatever management system is put in place, and whatever content is reviewed, measured, and discussed, is what will become the focus for the organization. It follows the saying, "what gets measured gets done." If management is focused on it, everyone else will be too. A well-designed management system will address strategy, translation of the strategy into work, operational planning, resource planning (capex, opex, people, and physical resources) and regular monitoring of execution. The management system promotes accountability through transparency and knowledge sharing. By participating in the management system, people learn about what's working and what's not working, and the organizational ecosystem can be adapted dynamically. Through that adaptation, the workforce is constantly encouraged to take a forward view of the business. Without a well-designed management system to promote forward progress, management efforts inevitably end up getting bogged down with a backwards-looking view: examining the financials and operational metrics of past performance.

Systems both enable and control the execution of tasks and decisions. As a matter of fact, one of the best ways to ensure process adoption is to systematize the process steps wherever possible. One of the best ways to ensure effective decision making is to codify the decision in a system. Systems *can* be tools, and tools *can* be systems, but the two are not mutually inclusive; therefore, when trying to effect performance changes in the organizational ecosystem, each should be given due consideration. Let's look at a few examples of how to systematize a desired performance change and process.

Royce's Machine Shop uses a hydraulic press to form sheet metal. The press has been identified as a safety hazard because workers could choose to hold on to a piece of metal while activating the press. There are 3 disciplines at play here: decision making, process, and systemization. We want to eliminate the ability of the coworker to be able to make a decision to place their hands inside the press while activating it. You could have a meeting with the workers and formally address their *decision rights*, clarifying that they do not have the *authority* to decide to place their hands in the press while activating it. You could facilitate a *process* workshop where everyone maps out a new operating process for the press, which explicitly requires a step to remove all body parts before activating it. Ultimately, *systemization* is essential for effectively removing the risk of injury in this case. A discussion with the workers is still warranted, and discussing the *decision rights* and *process* should be part of it. What's really wanted is to change the *process* for how the press is operated, and it's necessary to *systematize* that process so that it must be followed or the press won't function. Installing machine interlocks is the *systemization* that prevents potential injury. The systemized interlocks require a worker to step away from the machine, place each of their hands on a button while simultaneously stepping on a lever that activates the press. The only way this *systemization* could be bypassed is through an intentional act of defiance by one or more people. All three, process, decision rights, and systemization, are part of the solution, but *systemization* makes it *stick*.

Let's look at another example. Marcy's retail company has hundreds of locations around the world, and timely hiring is vital to effective operation. However, they currently route requisition requests manually through paper and email. It takes a long time; requests get lost in email, and there are several levels of approval that are necessary. Not everyone who should be approving actually does, and not everyone who should be made aware of new requisitions knows that they've been approved (or denied.) There are 4 disciplines at play here: *Decision rights* and approval levels need to be defined, *process*/work flow needs to be mapped, a *tool* needs to be selected/used to facilitate the workflow, and *systemization* needs to be applied. It is the *systemization* that ensures the rest are completed as desired. In this example, Marcy's may choose to use their Enterprise Resource Planning (ERP) system to facilitate a requisition process and automatic routing and escalation of approvals. The ERP system performs hundreds of functions; this is an example of where the *system* and the *tool* are the same.

A final example for systemization is an older one, to show that systemization has been around for a long time. To ensure physical security of facilities, security guards go on regular patrol routes. In a factory setting, where facilities cover acres, a patrol route can take quite a bit of time to complete. The route is usually perimeter based and the guards need to check that entry points (e.g. doors, windows, docks, etc.) are secure. A couple of problems inevitably arise: How do you ensure that all points have been checked on every route? How do you know that the guard is walking the patrol versus hiding in a closet taking a nap? Hence, the use of sentry boxes. Today we use radios, cell phones, and other location devices/services, but step back a few decades and sentry boxes were all the rage. A sentry box is a box that is mounted at/near each key checkpoint on a patrol route. After walking a route segment and checking the entry points, a guard would have to open the box with a key and flip a switch or push a button to register the box. Each activation would be tracked at a central control station. This *systemization* includes the use of physical, mechanical, and electronic means to ensure the performance of a *process* and tasks. (An even older, age-old, method was the deposit and pick-up of "chits" which were numbered for each station. You were either on a route where you were depositing "chits" or picking up "chits." The accountability was with the next person who went on the patrol.)

In these examples, you can enact any/all of the disciplines to try to solve the problems. The point of using an ecosystem view is that you select those disciplines that will correlate to the desired change in performance, and in most situations, it requires multiple disciplines. Royce's machine shop could have used incentives to try to motivate people to keep their hands out of the machines, but systemization and subsequent prevention is the better choice. Marcy's retail company could have reorganized to try to eliminate layers of approval, but the higher correlation to performance improvement is with process streamlining and systemization. To ensure physical security of factories, one could take a people approach and staff every point of entry with a person, but that would be costly and still doesn't ensure that security guards are awake and paying attention. The approach of systematizing the checkpoints solves the need more efficiently.

Tools enable the performance of tasks. The word "tools" invokes a lot of different meanings, and rightfully so. A tool could be something as simple as a pencil to something as complex as an interstellar spaceship. There are a couple questions to ask when considering tools which will help frame your thinking: Do people have the right tools to do the jobs they're being asked to do? Are our people using the tools most effectively? Proper tools selection enables both effective and efficient completion of a job.

Take for example the previous request for a sales force realignment. The business needed to drive consistent spans (opex and people resource utilization) between regions. One region was running a manager to salesperson ratio of 1:16, while another region was running a ratio of 1:8. The higher span region was equally effective, and the executive leadership team wanted to capitalize on the efficiencies. From three managerial layers away, that makes complete sense; however, the larger span of one region was enabled by a defined sales methodology and toolset. Each sales person used formal tools to plan and manage their territory and every customer-call that they conducted. Because of the tools, and the skill development that went with them, the sales force required less managerial oversight. The smaller span region was not able to get the funding for the tools or training. Organizational structure was part of the final and desired solution, but a toolset was needed to enable the changes.

Another very different tool example was a factory that produced steel shutters and awnings. The final assembly area of the factory was having throughput problems that seemed to coincide with a managerial change that took place six months earlier. The factory director was requesting both an organizational and personnel change to correct the performance issue. During a focus group meeting with the workers, the question was posed directly to them, "what's causing the poor performance the past six months?" Their response was unanimous: the new air impact wrenches. Early in the year the procurement team negotiated new pricing on air tools, but in order to get the pricing they needed to standardize the toolset so they would have a larger volume purchase. The factory had previously used five different types of air impact wrenches. The performance degradation was present throughout the factory, but it was most egregious during this final stage of manufacturing. It had such a significant impact at this stage because these workers had to use the air impact wrenches 100% of the time. Every step that they performed required their use. The tool was not designed for 100% duty cycle, and so it was wearing out rapidly. Whereas, in other parts of the factory, the same air impact wrench was one of several tools used, and it was used on a periodic basis. The new manager had tried to get the old air impact wrenches ordered, but she was overridden by procurement. In the focus group she said point blank, "We wear these out in a few days, and then we're not allowed to order new ones until the next month. You get me the right tool and performance will improve immediately." An examination of the production reports confirmed it: the first week of every month (new tools) the performance was good, and the next three weeks it progressively declined. In this example, an organizational and managerial change was not needed. Tool and procurement process changes were needed.

People fill jobs, which are composed of a set of tasks that need to be performed. The combination of organizational structure, decision rights, processes, systems, and tools work together to define the division of labor and the job content. People need to be in jobs that are substantive and meaningful, and they need to possess the right compliment of knowledge, skills, and attitudes to perform the jobs effectively and efficiently. Everything that is done in the people discipline is about ensuring that people are in jobs that are a good fit for them. Many of the functions of human capital management (HCM) and human resources (HR) rally around this mission.

The areas of talent acquisition, talent management, learning and development, and employee relations all contribute directly to ensuring that a company has the right people/job alignment. Talent acquisition works to fill open positions. Talent management ensures internal people resources can be dynamically mobilized to meet business needs, and it does this through development and organizational visibility of the people resources. Learning and development bridges gaps in knowledge, skills, and attitudes by providing timely access to learning, skill modeling and practice, and behavioral coaching. Employee relations provides a critical feedback loop and identifies when things are not working optimally. The remaining HCM/HR functions are focused on either incentives or compliance.

Incentives provide the motivation for people to perform tasks the way that the company desires. The watersheds of incentives are rooted

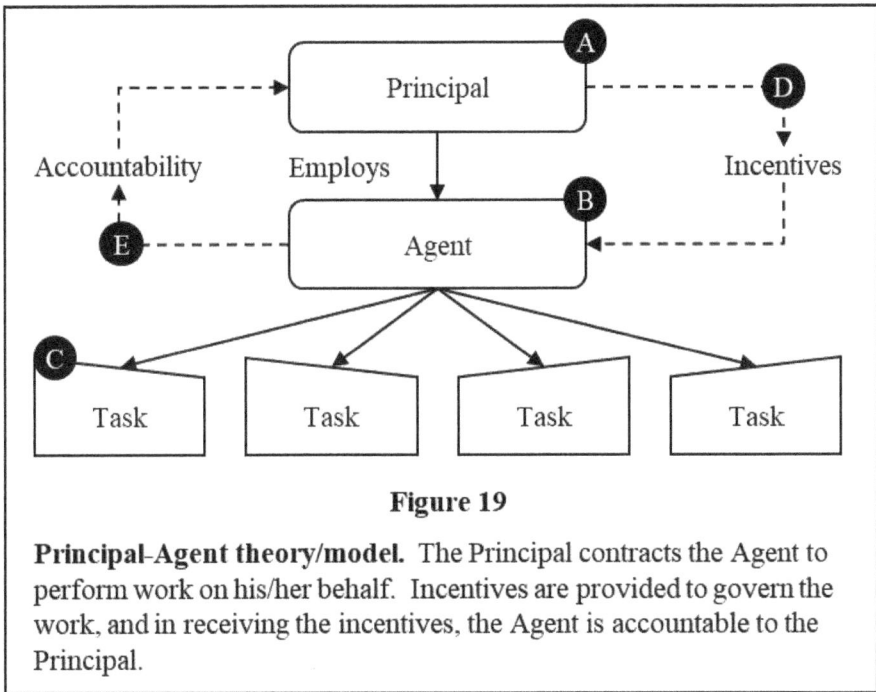

Figure 19

Principal-Agent theory/model. The Principal contracts the Agent to perform work on his/her behalf. Incentives are provided to govern the work, and in receiving the incentives, the Agent is accountable to the Principal.

in what's known as the agency dilemma. As Figure 19 illustrates, agency dilemma arises when someone needs to enlist the support of another person to accomplish work on their behalf; the former becomes the principal (A) and the latter becomes the agent (B). The agent

performs tasks (C) on behalf of the principal. The dilemma develops around the inability of the principal to *perfectly control* the actions of the agent. In a perfect-control situation, the agent would perform the work in precisely the manner that the principal desires.

The premise of the agency dilemma is that, in human relations, *perfect control* cannot be achieved; therefore, mechanisms are put in place that strive for the *most*-perfect-control possible. Payment (D) for services performed is a fundamental mechanism that is used to motivate and control the agent. In exchange for receipt of payment, the agent submits to accountability (E) with the principal. Providing incentives and establishing accountability does <u>not</u> yield *perfect control* though, and that is the number one challenge in the space of compensation and incentives.

Additionally, the mere act of employing an agent creates a knowledge gap between the agent and principal. Because of delegation, the agent is in closer proximity to the tasks being performed; therefore, the agent possesses knowledge that the principal does not. Mentioned previously, the knowledge gap is known in the research by the term *information asymmetry*, meaning that the knowledge possessed by the agent, in comparison to the principal, is asymmetrical in nature and cannot be fully known by the principal. The greater the number of agents and the greater the number of layers in the organization, the greater the information asymmetry and resultant knowledge gap.

The description of the agency dilemma, and the associated depiction in Figure 19, are a simplistic representation. Degrees of separation compound and multiply information asymmetry, and incentives are a limited control mechanism. In other words, it is *one* of the disciplines needed to effect performance change in the organizational ecosystem. It is more powerful when used in a multi-disciplinary manner.

Making changes in the three areas (Figure 15-C) of organizational capability, value discipline, and product/services will impact the effectiveness and efficiency of the company. There are seven disciplines (Figure 15-E) that can be leveraged to drive changes in the organizational ecosystem, and they are best applied in a multi-disciplinary manner. To propel the company forward, it's imperative to take into account the whole of the business, and then to select the disciplines with the highest correlation to success.

Summary

Making changes to a business ecosystem to drive performance improvements requires a multi-disciplinary approach. The 7 disciplines are each amazingly important as levers to impact how a business functions. Each of the 7 disciplines are also interdependent. Organizational design *that sticks* leverages all of the disciplines to drive ecosystem improvements.

Leveraging Multiple Disciplines

Chapter Focus

One of the most important concepts in this book for improving performance, is that the 7 disciplines are *interdependent*. The IRA-7 approach is described along with how to select and use the 7 disciplines. Each of the 7 are process mapped, including organizational design.

Organizational design *that sticks* is rarely accomplished through the execution of a single discipline. To put in place an organizational structure that *sticks* requires a focus on the variables that most contribute to improved business performance. To effect performance, this is rarely done by driving change in only one part of a business. Business performance improvement *that sticks* works in multiple areas to affect changes to the overall operation of the ecosystem. The best reason for using multiple disciplines is that it embodies systems thinking, which has been shown to have higher correlation to improved performance.

The larger the business and the more complex the interactions, the more important it is to evaluate the relationships between IOC's, value chain functions, and the seven disciplines. A model, shown in Figure 20, called IRA-7 helps address business performance issues by *choosing* the disciplines to apply, based on an expectation of their ability to impact performance. One of the most important concepts in this book, the most critical for improving performance, is

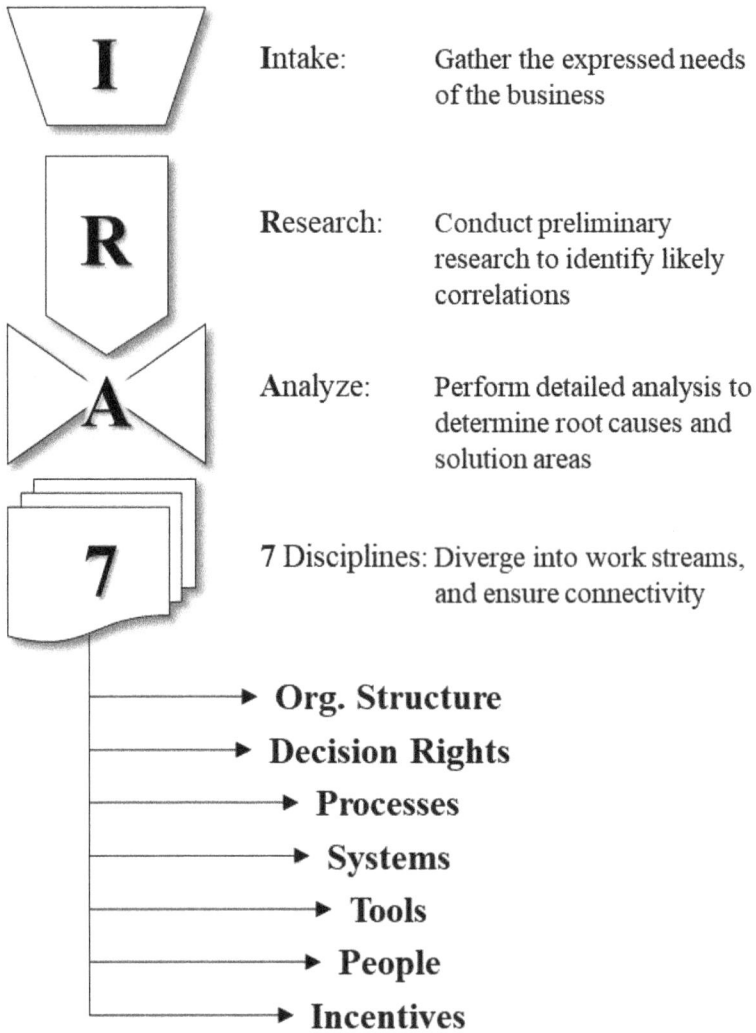

Intake: Gather the expressed needs of the business

Research: Conduct preliminary research to identify likely correlations

Analyze: Perform detailed analysis to determine root causes and solution areas

7 Disciplines: Diverge into work streams, and ensure connectivity

Org. Structure

Decision Rights

Processes

Systems

Tools

People

Incentives

Figure 20

IRA-7. Designing for the benefit of the ecosystem requires an approach that intentionally performs Intake, Research, Analysis, and uses the 7 disciplines to drive overall performance improvement. Each discipline has its own methodology and body of knowledge to draw from.

that **the disciplines are** *interdependent.* It is because of this *interdependency*, that IRA-7 is so useful.

The selection among the seven disciplines should be done in the context of understanding the forces that are at work on the business, and intentionally choosing to change those components that have the highest impact on performance. This is the most powerful outcome of systems thinking: sustained improvement of output in both effectiveness and efficiency. Sustained improvements are accomplished by intentional and planned use of multiple disciplines. Through the application of the seven disciplines, a business works on multiple systemic variables simultaneously, each contributing in part to performance improvements, and all contributing together for holistic ecosystem improvements.

Each discipline shown in Figure 20 has its own methodology, and each discipline varies in depth and complexity. For example, an entire industry (IT) exists to address *systems*, and there are multiple career paths with degree programs, professional associations, and certifications. In contrast, *organizational design* is more of a specialty skill and practice area. To be great at organizational design takes years of study and practice. There are a few degree programs and certifications, but there are no standards or governing bodies that formalize the discipline. One could look at the *tools* discipline and think that there's very little to say about it; however, it's arguably the biggest body of work among all seven disciplines. Tools are pervasive in every industry, every profession, and every trade.

An earlier chapter explained the *organizational design* process, shown again in Figure 21. These engagements typically follow a six-step process. To leverage another discipline, it's necessary to understand the overall process *that* discipline follows. Organizational design engagements often couple together with *decision rights* engagements because the organizational structure addresses the formal

Needs	Diagnose	Design	Linkages	Select	Implement

Process Steps

Figure 21

Organizational Design Process. The six-step process for conducting organizational design engagements.

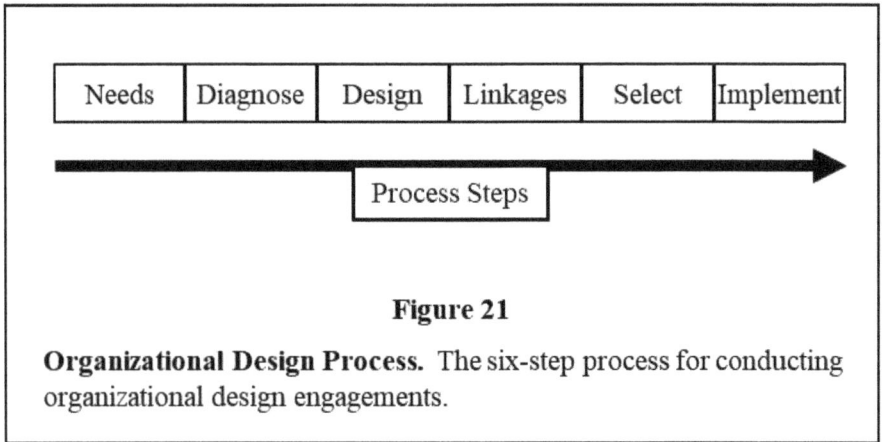

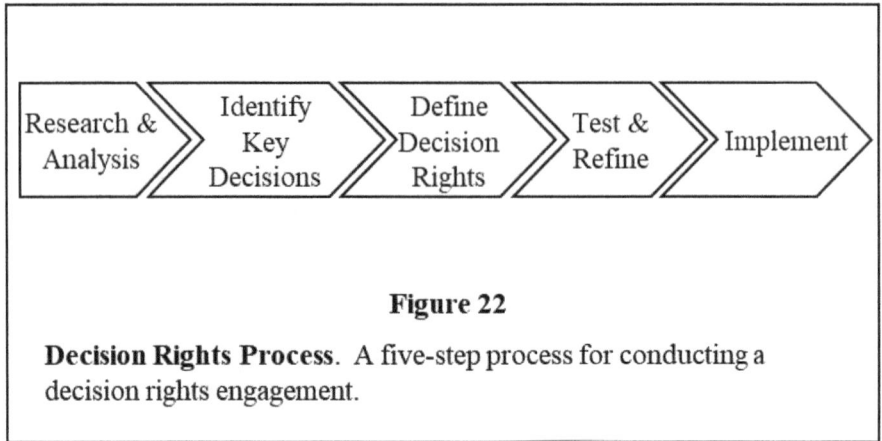

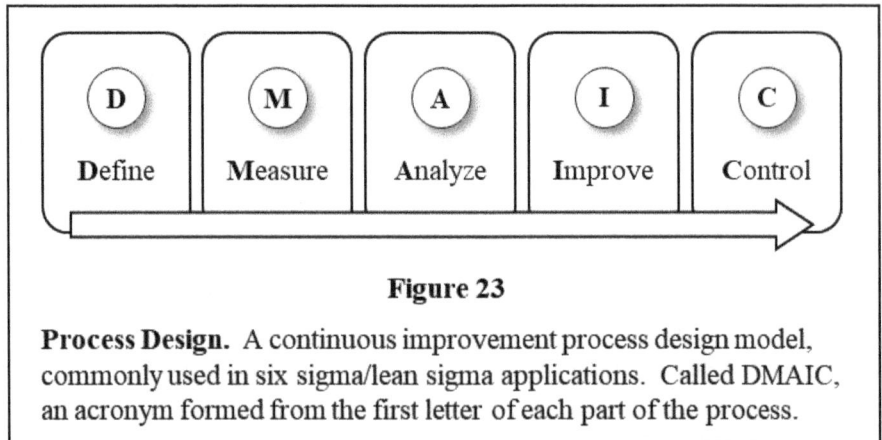

Research & Analysis > Identify Key Decisions > Define Decision Rights > Test & Refine > Implement

Figure 22

Decision Rights Process. A five-step process for conducting a decision rights engagement.

D Define	**M** Measure	**A** Analyze	**I** Improve	**C** Control

Figure 23

Process Design. A continuous improvement process design model, commonly used in six sigma/lean sigma applications. Called DMAIC, an acronym formed from the first letter of each part of the process.

structures, and the decision rights address what is typically an informal power structure. The decision rights engagement process is shown in Figure 22. This process has five-steps. There are similarities and differences between the organizational design and decision rights processes. If one needed to couple these together with a *process design* engagement, as shown in Figure 23, the differences become even more noticeable. The process design approach comes from the six sigma/lean sigma practice area, and the one shown here is a continuous improvement model.

Because of the variability between the bodies of work for each of the disciplines, the first challenge in leveraging them is understanding them. While each discipline varies, there are commonalities that can be exercised. Doing so, allows one to save time and resources, and it drives performance improvement and higher success rates. Figure 24 takes each of the seven disciplines and maps their respective high-level processes side-by-side. Across the top is an overlay of IRA-7 and a process flow that has been generalized into the following nine steps:

The first three steps are IRA, which stand for Intake, Research, and Analyze. One of the primary goals of IRA is to make a selection among the seven disciplines that will provide the highest correlation for improving business performance.

1. **Intake:** Several of the disciplines use an intake step where the practitioner collects information related to perceived needs, issues, and concerns.

2. **Research:** Most of the disciplines contain a step for research. This is where qualitative and quantitative instruments are built and used to better understand the performance concerns. Extant data collection is also performed during this step.

3. **Analyze:** All the disciplines use an analysis step where information is reviewed and assessed. The information is

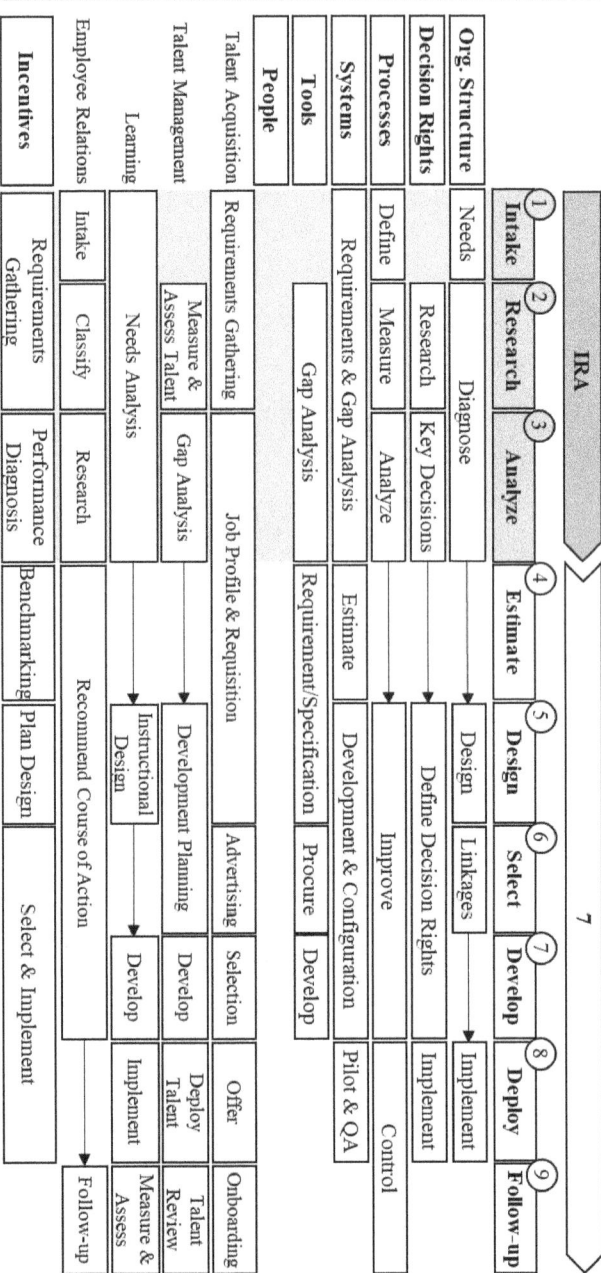

IRA

Discipline	1 Intake	2 Research	3 Analyze	4 Estimate	5 Design	6 Select	7 Develop	8 Deploy	9 Follow-up
Org. Structure	Needs	Diagnose	Key Decisions		Design	Linkages		Implement	
Decision Rights	Define	Research			Define Decision Rights			Implement	
Processes	Define	Measure	Analyze			Improve		Control	
Systems	Requirements & Gap Analysis			Estimate	Development & Configuration			Pilot & QA	
Tools	Gap Analysis			Requirement/Specification	Procure		Develop		
People									
Talent Acquisition	Requirements Gathering			Job Profile & Requisition	Advertising	Selection	Offer	Onboarding	
Talent Management	Measure & Assess Talent		Gap Analysis		Development Planning		Develop	Deploy Talent	Talent Review
Learning	Needs Analysis				Instructional Design		Develop	Implement	Measure & Assess
Employee Relations	Intake	Classify	Research			Recommend Course of Action			Follow-up
Incentives	Requirements Gathering	Performance Diagnosis	Benchmarking		Plan Design		Select & Implement		

A

Figure 24

IRA-7. The combined work processes of the 7 disciplines.

put together to show correlations, cause-effect, and to discern root-causes of the performance issue(s).

It's these first three steps that present the most opportunity to leverage work, identified in Figure 24-A. While the body of work associated with each discipline calls the steps something different, their net outcome is intended to be the same: identify the root cause(s) of the performance gap(s).

The primary weakness of approaching business performance issues through only one discipline is that you'll always find a problem. Unfortunately, each discipline, when enacted by itself tends to *find itself* as a need…it becomes a self-fulfilling prophecy. In other words, if one goes looking for an organizational structure problem, one is likely to find some. Likewise, if one goes looking for systems problems, one is likely to find some. None of our business ecosystems are perfect, not in any company or in any industry; therefore, if you go looking for problems in any of these seven disciplines, you're likely to find them.

The better way to approach solving a business performance issue is to perform the front-end intake, research, and analysis with all seven disciplines in mind. By doing so, the practitioner, is truly problem solving and is not predisposed to creating work in any one discipline by itself. When done in this manner, estimation (Figure 24 - Step 4) becomes a necessary step for all disciplines; whereas, by themselves, few of the disciplines prescribe such a step.

4. **Estimate:** Collects the analyses and puts forward a proposal for solving the business performance gap, along with an estimate of the resources required.

It is from this point forward that the disciplines diverge into parallel work streams, the "7" portion of IRA-7. Each discipline works to effect its changes on the business ecosystem. Sequencing and regular connection between the work streams is necessary for the future step of deployment. There are often dependencies that need to be taken into account between the work streams. For example, new decision rights are often dependent upon both organizational structure and process changes.

5. **Design**	
6. **Select**	Each of the design, select, develop,
7. **Develop** ⬅	deploy, and follow-up steps are
8. **Deploy**	performed according to the body of
9. **Follow-up**	knowledge for each discipline.

Let's look at an example application with a computer systems and network design company. The company was ten years old, and they had grown to operate in about 30 States. They aspired to grow to a national company in the next three years. To this point, they operated with a centralized corporate structure where they did all their design and build work. They had a three-region field structure which included geographically dispersed resources for sales, and technical resources for deployments.

For convenience/reference, the ecosystem chart has been repeated in Figure 25. The company's inputs (Figure 25-A) include computer and networking components, both hardware and software. The inputs also include associated accessories and third-party applications. They produce (Figure 25-B) system architecture designs, which they install, configure, optimize, and turn over to clients. They lead in the market (Figure 25-C) through product/system designs which are customized to customer needs. The company is optimized for organizational capabilities (Figure 25-C, D) in supplier sourcing, IT-systems architecture, IT-hardware and software configurations, and operations for deployment. Marketing and sales focus on mid-large market companies in business-to-business transactions which are exclusively done through a proposal-bid and quote process.

Following IRA-7, Figure 20, during the *intake* step, the situation was one where competitors were making fast inroads against market-share based on service. The company was losing bids due to

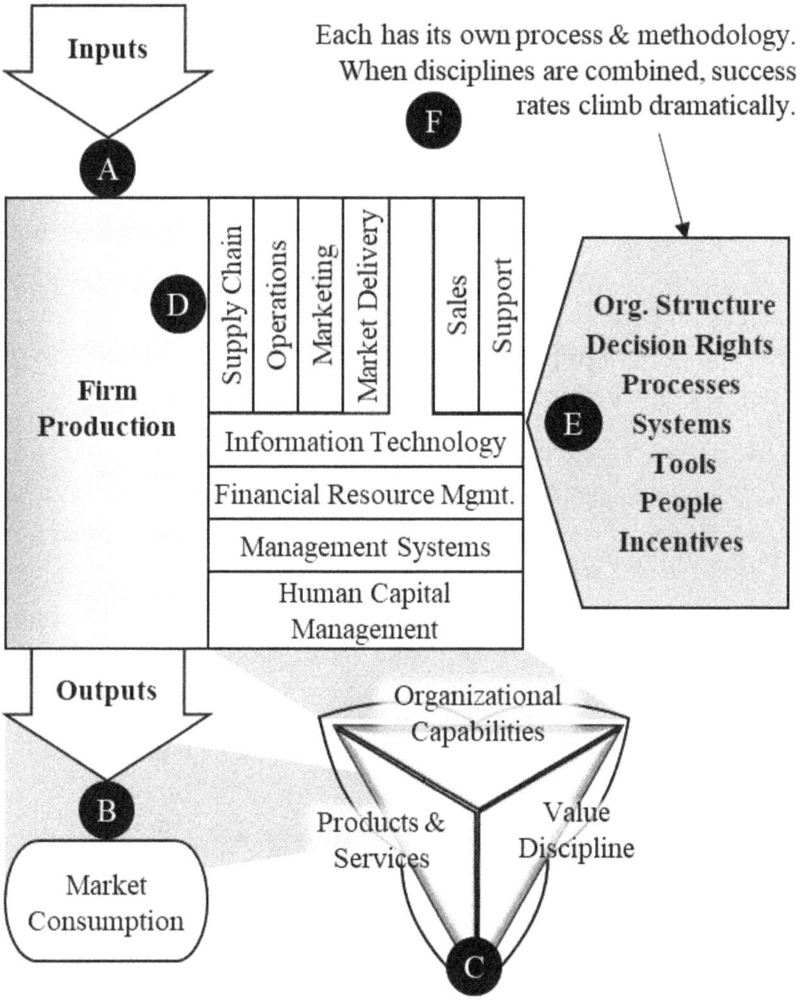

Inputs

Each has its own process & methodology.
When disciplines are combined, success
rates climb dramatically.

F

A

D

| Supply Chain | Operations | Marketing | Market Delivery | | Sales | Support |

**Firm
Production**

**Org. Structure
Decision Rights
Processes
Systems
Tools
People
Incentives**

E

Information Technology

Financial Resource Mgmt.

Management Systems

Human Capital
Management

Outputs

B

Market
Consumption

Organizational
Capabilities

Products &
Services

Value
Discipline

C

Figure 25

Business Eco-System and Multi-Disciplinary Approach:
Adapted from Porter's Five Forces, Porter, M.E. (1990). *The
competitive advantage of nations*. New York, NY: Free Press. Also
adapted from Value Disciplines, Tearcy, M. & Wiersema, F. (1995).
The Disciplines of Market Leaders. New York, NY: Harper Collins
Publishers, Inc.

competitors having better customer service and post-install support. While the company's product design capability was still a differentiator, and they believed it would continue to be, it was not enough to maintain the win-rates they had historically gotten and that they continued to want and need. It was believed that product leadership was still the way to go, but they needed to make an investment in support so that it was not a detractor. Improved support *capability* was viewed as a need for their continued growth strategy to become a national provider. The request was to facilitate an organizational design project to determine where they needed to make changes in their organizational structure.

Qualitative *research* was conducted that included one-on-one interviews with leaders, and focus groups in support and sales. Selected customers were also interviewed. Quantitative *research* was conducted by reviewing survey data from customers for the previous five years. One of the key outputs from the research was the identification of 5 key performance indicators (KPIs) in two areas. Shown in Figure 26, they are:

- **Improving Opex Efficiencies:** Operational expenditures were quickly identified by the leadership team. The regional leaders were especially aware of the disparities between their budgets and spend levels. This had been a topic of many leadership meetings. There were three KPIs in this area:

  o **Align human resources ratios between regions:** The resource levels in each region varied widely. Historically, this evolved from projects that were won/delivered over time. The regions that had more historical activity had more resources, even though the resource levels didn't match their current or projected workloads.

  o **Establish consistent roles globally:** Several of their customers had multi-state or national presence. The company's installation leadership team was always assigned

	Org. Structure	Decision Rights	Process	Systems	Tools	People	Incentives	Total
Improve Opex Efficiencies								
Align human resource ratios	5	3	25	43	15	8	1	100
Establish consistent roles globally	27	5	25	4	11	28	0	100
Consolidate vendors	0	72	21	3	4	0	0	100
Improve Customer Service								
Drive service level globally	32	7	19	18	17	3	4	100
Shorten ticket resp. time globally	0	0	31	26	14	21	8	100
	64	87	121	94	61	60	13	

Figure 26

Interdependencies of the 7 disciplines: Sample scoring matrix where the 7 disciplines were scored according to their expected impact on the key performance indicators (KPIs).

based on the region that was closest to customers' headquarters. However, the site installations were distributed based on geographic location. Customers were confused because role-content varied between regions, and they were constantly having to figure out who does what.

o **Consolidate vendors:** Each region was procuring installation parts, accessories, consumables, tools, and other supply items on their own. In many cases, installation crews were shopping these items at retailers that were close to installation sites.

- **Improving Customer Service:** This area was also quickly identified by leadership, and it was expressly called out by the customers that were interviewed. The research revealed two KPIs that needed to be addressed:

o **Driving service levels "globally":** Customer ratings on service levels varied substantially between regions and additionally by type of project. In situations where the projects were solely design, and the customers did their own deployment, the company scored very well. Where the projects included field deployment, the scores varied by region. Defining this as a "global" KPI meant that the company wanted to drive consistent scores across all their geographies.

o **Shortening service request/ticket response times "globally":** This KPI was feedback that came directly from customers. The company had been working on a 48-hour response time; whereas, customer expectations were within an 8-hour workday.

The off-line analysis and facilitated group workshops revealed the linkages shown in Figure 26. The effort needed to improve opex and customer service was not just organizational design. Organizational design was part of the solution, but so were *five* of the other disciplines! It took *6* of the *7* disciplines to enact the changes that the company needed. What's shown in Figure 26 is the outcome of a very useful exercise, taking into account all of the seven disciplines. The participants were asked to score each KPI (Figure 26-A) by distributing 100 points between the seven disciplines. They assigned the most points to the discipline that would contribute the most to improving the KPI, and they could assign any point value from 0-100. The scoring was done horizontally (Figure 26-A) by each KPI. All participant scores were collected, the results were compiled and then averaged. At that point, a summary by discipline was tallied (Figure 26-B) so that the team could see the resultant point value of each discipline.

The team scoring demonstrates that achieving the performance improvements that the company needed was a multi-disciplinary effort that impacted the business ecosystem. The work streams for each discipline were mapped out in a work breakdown structure so that dependencies and timing could be fully vetted. From an organizational design perspective, this was very important. The team that worked through the organizational design, put together what the future state should look like, but the deployment of that future state lagged by 7 months. During those 7 months, other teams worked through process, system, and tool changes that would enable the new structure. Then, all were deployed in a synchronized manner.

It is difficult to imagine how the company would have completed the effort had it been done in a more "traditional" manner. In a "traditional" manner, the request to conduct an organizational design project would have been met with eagerness. The consulting firm would have done some organizational research and analysis and determined that organizational changes were needed. Potential new structures would have been designed, and one would have been selected by the company's leadership. Then, organizational changes would have been made. Those changes would have been put in place without the necessary enabling work from the other disciplines. The consultancy would have walked away, pocketed thousands of dollars, and the company would be happy…for a little while. Until, of course, their customer service performance didn't improve during the next round of surveying…or the round after that…or the round after that. When the performance didn't improve, they would have looked at the newly hired leader, and their team, as being non-performers. Then, 12-18 months after the organizational change, they would likely make leadership changes, which would also require more organizational changes. Therein lies the negative reinforcing loop of organizational redesigns and the cause of failure rates that range from 60-70%.

> Multi-disciplinary efforts solve the performance issues systemically, and they do so the first time around. They take more planning, more coordination, and a little more patience. As the saying goes, "anything worth doing is worth doing right the first time."

This is a good point to address two professions (skill areas) that are highly useful and beneficial: Project Management and Change Management. Project management is a temporary endeavor which drives execution. It does so by applying a formal approach to planning, scheduling, managing people and financial resources, and controlling and mitigating adjustments along the way. Change management is also a temporary endeavor which drives adoption with employees. It does so by applying a formal approach to gap analyses, change preparation, communication, training, and follow-up. Either or both professions could be performed by permanent/internal resources within a company. The availability of them, as internal resources, depends on the nature of the work the company performs and the size/maturity of the organization. Large and mature companies tend to have internal resources in these professions. Small and mid-market companies often do not have these resources, and procuring them from an external source is a good approach.

Applying both project and change management helps ensure execution and success. Planning and coordination between the disciplines and work streams is a must: the outputs of each work stream must be timed with each other. Their dependencies must be understood and sequenced. Furthermore, a full resource view is needed; many times, the same people are used in multiple discipline's work streams, and these people still need to perform their "day jobs." Anticipating, identifying, and documenting changes across the work streams is also a must. The working team members will have direct knowledge of the changes, but they are often too focused on the content of the changes (rightfully so,) and having a dedicated resource work on the change impacts is vital for adoption.

Summary

Organizational design *that sticks* is accomplished through the execution of multiple disciplines. To put in place an organizational structure *that sticks* requires a focus on the variables that most contribute to improved business performance. Driving performance improvements requires a full understanding of the business ecosystem and working intentionally on all 7 disciplines that impact how the organization operates. All 7 disciplines can share up-front work using the IRA-7 model to perform intake, research, and analysis. Then, the work streams can diverge into their separate disciplines. It is vital though that they remain coordinated and connected to each other, so that their outputs can be timed for maximum impact and adoption.

Major Ecosystem Events

Chapter Focus

There are a few common and significant ecosystem events that companies encounter. These include vertical integration, horizontal integration, and outsourcing. This chapter examines the impact these have on the business ecosystem and their organizational design implications.

There are a few major ecosystem events that warrant some additional treatment from an organizational design standpoint. Those events include vertical integration, horizontal integration, and outsourcing. This chapter, will examine each of these along with some examples.

Vertical integration is when a company expands its products/services upstream or downstream in its supply chain. An upstream vertical integration involves taking over the products/services of a supplier. A downstream vertical integration involves taking over the products/services of a distributor. Vertical integration can be accomplished through acquisition, and it can be accomplished through organic growth by building additional organizational capabilities. Both have organizational design/structure implications, and both have business ecosystem implications.

Fully integrated vertical businesses are uncommon, with steel manufacturers and oil companies being notable examples. Steel is an example that has been around for a while, so most are somewhat familiar with the industry. Figure 27 provides a simple view of the

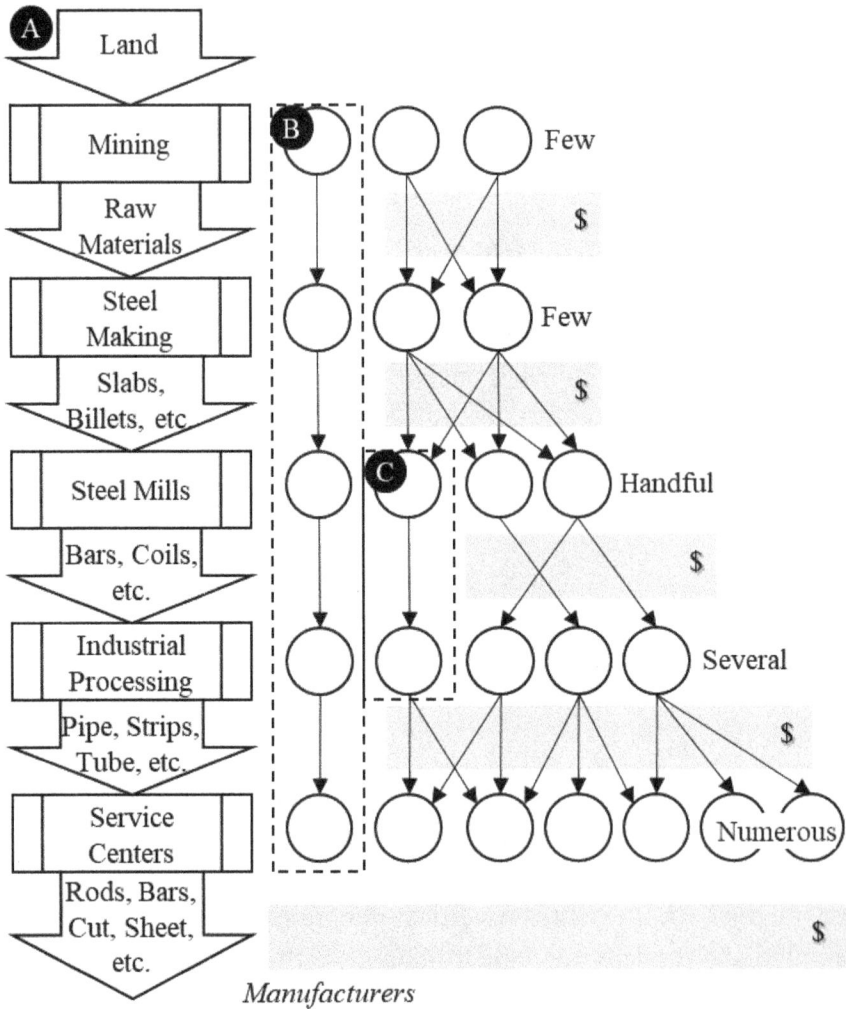

Figure 27

Vertical Integration: Using a high-level depiction of the steel industry, this illustration shows how vertical integration can be performed.

steel value chain. In this illustration, there are five distinct production steps shown through the series of inputs, production, and outputs (Figure 27-A.) In order to mine for raw materials, the mining production needs land with associated mineral rights as its input. It produces, as its output, raw materials such as iron ore and limestone. These become inputs into the steel making production process. Steel making produces slabs and billets, and these become inputs for the milling process. The steel mills produce rods, plates, and sheets, and these become inputs for industrial processing. Industrial processing forms the rods, plates, or sheets into tubing, piping, coated steel, and wire products, and these become inputs for the service centers. Steel servicing does cutting, bending, and forming where it produces outputs such as wire rod, rebar, painted sheet, and other formed steel. These become inputs for manufacturers who further refine these steel products into consumer goods.

On the right side of Figure 27, the number of circles indicate a relative number of producers at each stage of the supply chain. In comparison to the rest of the supply chain, there are few mining operations compared to the numerous service centers. A full vertically-integrated steel company (Figure 27-B) controls every production stage of the supply chain. In this depiction, it produces for and supplies *itself*. A partial vertically-integrated steel company (Figure 27-C) controls the milling and industrial processing stages. The rest of the depiction assumes that each circle is a separate company, operating in an open and free flow of trade. Each shaded area with a dollar-sign, "$," indicates where profits are made along the supply chain.

As is the case in most supply chains, as one goes down the supply chain, there are more producers at each successive stage. This is due to a couple of primary factors, the principle being the barriers to entry. Raw material processing, early in the supply chain, tend to be more capital intensive, and raw materials tend to be more difficult to find and extract. Company "C" (Figure 27-C) is positioned in the middle of this supply chain. A vertical integration strategy could take them either upstream or downstream, and each has different implications. An upstream integration would mean acquiring the steel making capabilities of one of its current suppliers. If company "C" did this, and then constrained the output of the steel making to supply only itself, it would place further supply constraints on the steel making outputs of slabs, billets, etc. Constraining supply, while holding demand steady, would force prices up in the rest of the market. This would work to the advantage of company "C", as they would control their own steel making capabilities. Likewise, it would benefit company "B" (Figure 27-B) which is already vertically integrated. A downstream integration would mean acquiring a service center. If company "C" did this, it would not have the same supply constraint effect of an upstream acquisition. It may have such an effect within a defined geography; however, the most likely application of a downstream move like this would be to control the product dynamics of type, quality, cost, and speed of production.

The organizational implications of vertical integration are many. The entire business ecosystem in Figure 25 *can* be called into question. The more variables that are introduced, the greater the need for an ecosystem approach. While every combination and permutation of a vertical integration cannot be vetted here, it is useful to explore *one* so that the organizational design and human resources implications can be seen.

Continue with Figure 28, and Company "C" completing an upstream integration. When Company "C's" footprint is extended upstream, you'll notice that some of the transactions are erased. The former independent steel making company sold its products to several mills; however, those transactions have been reduced so that Company "C" can supply its own steel mills directly. Letter "D" and the dashed arrow indicates that they are still going to supply steel to another independent mill, and because of that, the pricing scheme will need to be addressed. As is often the case with vertical integrations, both external and internal pricing become a significant point of work and a

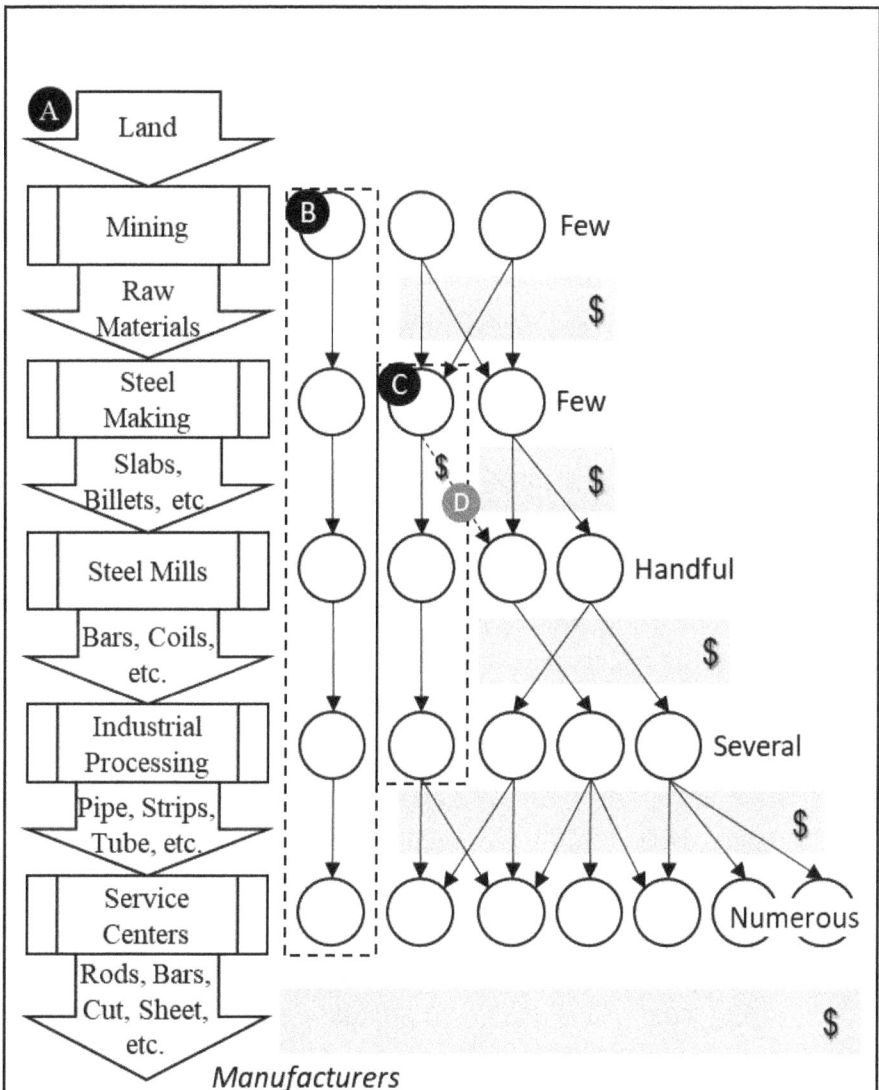

Figure 28

Vertical Integration: Using a high-level depiction of the steel industry, this illustration shows how vertical integration can be performed, with one company expanding upstream.

focus of *organizational capability*. The vertical integration inevitably means the acquisition of facilities, assets, and associated resources. Because these are discrete stages and distinct locations, the transfer of goods must still occur, even if it is within Company "C's" own boundaries. To facilitate this, transfer pricing is often used internally, while market pricing is used externally; this in-turn establishes an *organizational capability* need for cost accounting. Since Company "C" was already vertically integrated, it is likely that it already has some of this capability, but the acquired steel making company was not vertically integrated, so it may lack this capability. The resources associated with this between the pre-existing Company "C" and the acquired steel maker will need to be evaluated. Regarding *pricing*, each of the 7 disciplines may be impacted as follows:

- Organizational Structure: Addressing the location, size, and reporting of the pricing function between Company "C" and the acquired steel maker.

- Decision Rights: Defining who makes pricing decisions on internal transfer versus market sales will be necessary. Responsibilities need to be assigned for pricing analytics, proposals, and those who need to endorse the proposals before moving forward.

- Processes: The pricing process will need to be defined so the organization knows how to perform the work and how it will vary for internal and external pricing management. This will inevitably need to include accounting process changes, especially for the acquired steel maker.

- Systems: The financial and enterprise resource planning systems are impacted in terms of their use/licensing, deployment, configuration, access/authorities, and physical connectivity. Disparate systems and duplications will likely need to be rationalized.

- Tools: The tools area will need to be explored to determine if the company needs access to more sophisticated statistical tools for the pricing function. Additionally, there may be a combined tool and systems need so that the company can systemically collect needed information to enable accurate cost accounting.

- People: There will likely be a need to add, change, and remove people resources. Additions will come in skills that must be acquired immediately; for example, adding people with pricing and cost accounting skills at the acquired steel making facilities. Changing the skill make-up of people resources will likely also be required; for example, training accounting personnel at the acquired steel making facilities on the new financial and/or enterprise resource planning system. Removing people resources may also be considered; for example, those functions/departments where there are duplicative resources caused by the acquisition.

- Incentives: Proper pricing is important to Company "C." Internally, it means lowering the overall cost of its eventual output from its industrial processing centers, which provides it with better margins and/or better market pricing. Externally, it means that Company "C" will continue to earn revenue and profit from steel making. Designing and implementing aligned incentives so that pricing duties are performed effectively and transfer pricing works as designed is important.

There are many more implications to this example of upstream vertical integration. *Only the one around pricing was explored.* A quick brainstorm will yield others such as additional economies of scale for items like supplier agreements, employee benefits, logistics/distribution, traffic lanes, IT licensing, IT systems rationalizations, market and sales channels, and product support.

Referring to the ecosystem in Figure 25, the IOC's (C), the entire supply chain (D), and all 7 disciplines (E) are impacted by a vertical integration. It is vital to leverage IRA7 to drive the needed changes in the ecosystem and ensure adoption and success.

Horizontal Integration is when a company expands its production capacity and captures market at the same stage of the supply chain. Horizontal integration can be accomplished through acquisition, and it can be accomplished organically through building additional organizational capabilities. Both have organizational design/structure implications, and both have business ecosystem implications. Fully captured horizontal businesses are monopolies. They are therefore uncommon, and in most mature economies are illegal or highly regulated.

Continue with the previous example of the steel supply chain. Figure 29 introduces Company "E" growing from two service centers to four service centers. They are staying within their current supply chain stage and continuing to perform steel service center production; they produce steel rods, bars, sheets, and cutting. Pursuing horizontal integration allows them to capture more market share by acquiring a competitor and their locations, assets, and resources. Organically, a similar result can be achieved by opening new locations.

At first, the implications of horizontal integration would seem to be one of scaling, for either acquisition or organic growth. Using the latter approach of organic growth, the scaling implication is more likely true. Using the former approach and growing through acquisition presents additional implications. These additional implications come from the fact that no two companies are ever alike. As much as it is tempting to think so because they produce the same products, no two companies approach that production the same way. This is an application of the IOC's, shown again in Figure 30. While both companies may produce sheet steel, they will also likely produce

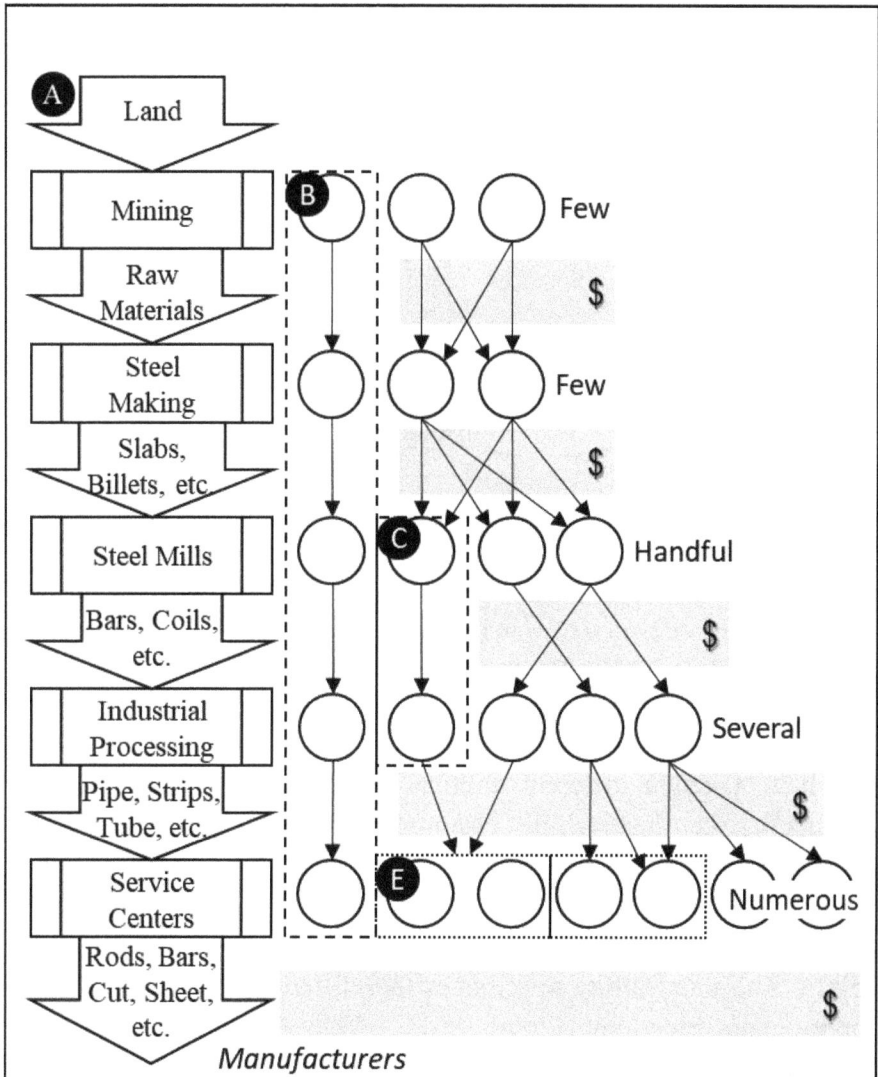

Figure 29

Horizontal Integration: Using a high-level depiction of the steel industry, this illustration shows how horizontal integration can be performed.

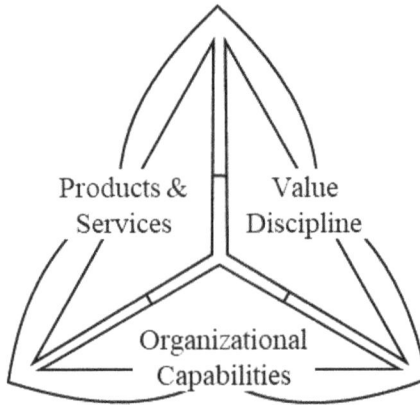

Figure 30

Interdependent Organizational Constructs (IOC's). The combination of these three constructs is what fills-out a firm's strategy and allows it to translate strategy into operational plans and objectives.

different sizes, thicknesses, finishes, and treatments. The companies will have taken a different approach to their value disciplines of product/service leadership, customer intimacy, and operational excellence. These will result in variations to customer service, product availability, customization, cycle time, pricing, and more. Each of these feeds a different makeup of organizational capabilities (Figure 25-C.) Those capability differences fuel different uses of each of the supply chain functions (Figure 25-D.) These would all need to be defined, their differences understood, and then intentional/strategic decisions made about what to retain versus change. Subsequently the 7 disciplines (Figure 25-E,) can be selected and applied using IRA7. Each of the 7 disciplines may be impacted as follows:

- Organizational Structure: A horizontal integration will usually see a fuller duplication of functions, especially the indirect functions of the value chain such as information technology, financial resource management, management systems, and human capital management. There is also a high probability that the direct functions will have some level of duplication. These duplications will need to be rationalized, while protecting the elements of the structures that provide the capabilities that enable *intended* variations in the value disciplines and products/services.

- Decision Rights: The most important decisions in a horizontal integration are the ones that determine products/services and value disciplines. These will drive organizational capabilities and the allocation of capex, opex, physical, and people resources.

- Processes, Systems, and Tools: These become highly interdependent in a horizontal integration. The degree of work largely depends on whether the acquired company will be "conformed" to the acquiring company or will it be "left alone" to service its customers/markets in the way it always has. If the acquired company is to be conformed, all processes, systems, and tools will need to be reviewed, rationalized, and optimized for the combined entity. If the acquired company is to be left alone, then only those processes, systems, and tools that they will share need to be reviewed.

- People: Unfortunately, one of the people implications is addressing duplicative resources. Most of this duplication will be found in the indirect value chain functions. Other implications include leveraging those human capital items that benefit from a larger scale such as benefits and other insurance products.

- Incentives: Establishing the incentive design that protects market strategy is critical. If the company desires to maintain the acquired company's product/service mix along with their value disciplines, the incentives for marketing, sales, and production (at a minimum) should reflect this retention. If the company desires to "conform" the acquired company to a single approach to products/services and value disciplines, then the incentives of all supply chain functions will need to be aligned with that transition.

The third and final major ecosystem event we'll examine is **outsourcing**. **Outsourcing** moves tasks, jobs, or entire departmental functions to an external third party, shown in Figure 31. As described throughout the book, inputs are taken into the value chain functions (Figure 31-A,) and the company converts them to outputs. In this example, the company has decided that payroll should be outsourced (Figure 31-B.) The underlying premise of outsourcing is that the company believes that it can obtain the work product/service more efficiently and effectively through an external transaction versus conducting it internally. Outsourcing has many implications to the ecosystem. Those implications are best addressed formally as part of the decision-making process. Some of those implications include the following:

- Outsourcing the work should not adversely impact the company's marketplace outputs. This is the most crucial factor for the company to consider. Every company produces market-value based on a set of products and services, and those are delivered with a mix of the value disciplines of product/service leadership, operational excellence, and customer intimacy. It is imperative to understand how outsourcing will impact the company's products and services and how they are viewed in the marketplace.

- To do the above, it is necessary to understand the change that outsourcing will have on the organization's capabilities. The adage is true that the ecosystem is perfectly designed to deliver the results that it's delivering. Outsourcing *anything*

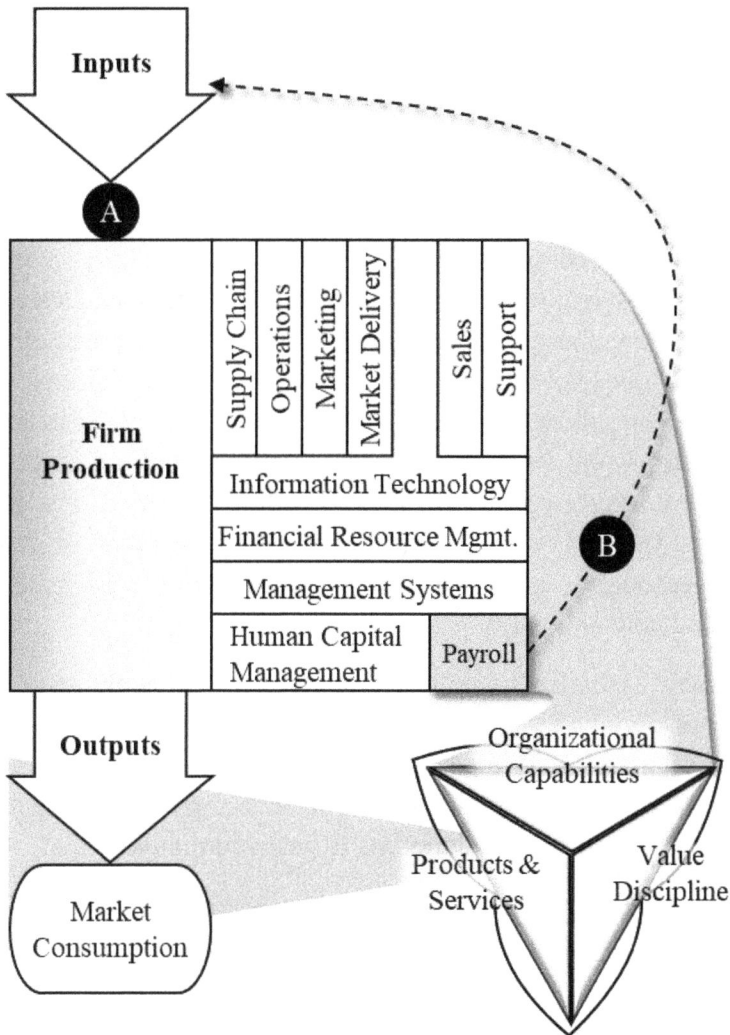

Figure 31

Outsourcing in the Ecosystem: Illustrates the net-effect of outsourcing in the business ecosystem.

will change the organizational capability mix. The question is, "How?"

Figure 32 shows a payroll outsourcing example and expands it to illustrate *some* of the organizational implications. A couple of the immediately perceived benefits of outsourcing is that the company gains a cost advantage in a couple ways. 1) The external outsourcer can perform the work more efficiently because it is their specialty, so both have the benefit of leveraging volume savings. Those savings can be passed through to the company. 2) Changes in financial statements: Because the company is not performing the function, it can eliminate the jobs and does not need to carry the costs of those positions. In the case of the payroll example, that means that the people resources are removed from the company's General/Administration costs. The outsourcer costs are carried on an expense line instead. Consequently, it reduces General/Administrative spend as a percent of revenue. Sounds reasonable, but the following implications will need to be understood and addressed:

- New capabilities are needed to effectively operate in an outsourcing relationship, indicated by "A" and the dashed line in Figure 32. While some of this may have already existed internally to the company, the outsourcing relationship now requires all of it be done in a formalized manner.

- Contracts and formal Service Level Agreements (SLAs) need to be established (Figure 32-B,) and this involves departments such as sourcing, procurement, and legal. None of these departments has *on-going* work requirements for the operation of payroll when it was performed internally by the company. When outsourced, both departments will have frequent and regular interaction with the outsourcer and the internal department that will manage the relationship, shown as human resources.

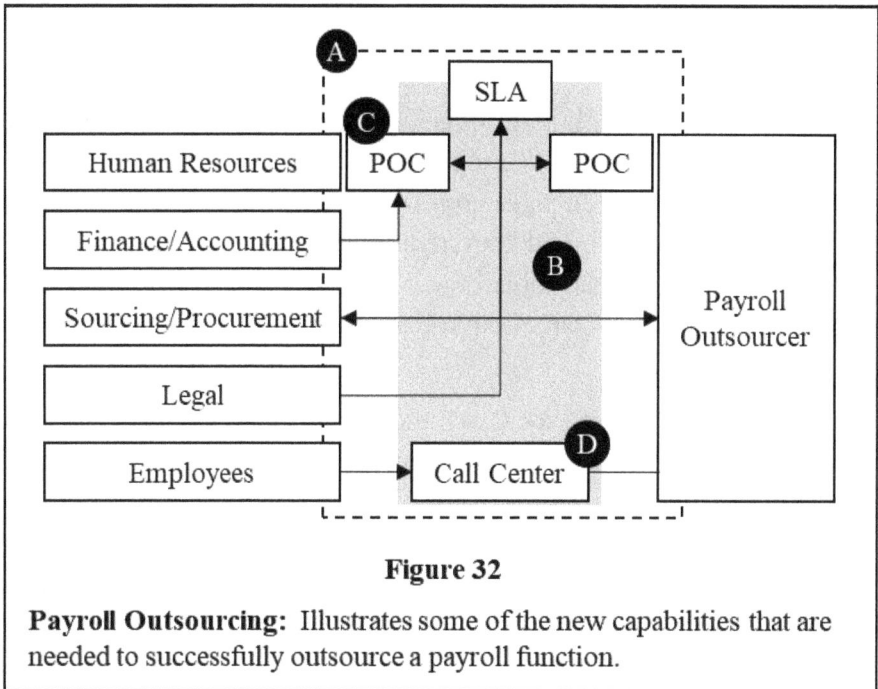

Figure 32

Payroll Outsourcing: Illustrates some of the new capabilities that are needed to successfully outsource a payroll function.

- The internal department that will manage the outsourced relationship will need to establish a Point-Of-Contact (POC) role (Figure 32-C.) This will be mirrored by the outsourcer. The performance of the payroll work will be overseen by these POC's, and the SLAs will govern the relationship.

- Employees have an interface to payroll (Figure 32-D.) When performed internally, that interface can be provided in a number of ways, and is often provided through multiple routes so employees can get their questions answered in an expedient manner (e.g. call their payroll representative, or call their HR manager.) The company and the outsourcer will need to negotiate a method for employee interface, and often this takes the shape of a call center, so the interaction becomes depersonalized. In many respects, that's the point of an external transaction versus an internally performed organizational capability: the company believes that they are better served by an external "depersonalized" transaction.

Nothing is "free" though; outsourcing comes with its own price. The formality of the outsourcing relationship removes flexibility. That's not to say that changes aren't possible, but inevitably, changes take time to negotiate, and they require pricing changes. The more programmatic and transactional the work, the easier it is to outsource; however, even in the case of payroll it's not something that should be considered lightly.

Payroll is one of the most commonly outsourced capabilities, but it's not as easy as it may first appear. It impacts at least 1 of the 7 disciplines, that the company needs to be able to use, to effect change on the ecosystem. The ability to dynamically define, implement, and execute incentives is critical to driving strategy and ensuring success. Being able to respond dynamically and to execute "creative" incentives is limited by the formality of the outsourced relationship. The outsourcer's capabilities also come into play. It's not uncommon to get a response that they are not able to implement an incentive design, either requiring changes to the incentive design and/or requiring contract/SLA changes. So, how important are incentives, and the ability of the payroll function to execute them?

Outsourcing essentially pushes a supply chain function into the realm of an *input* in the value chain. The payroll example is a relatively simple one. The complexities multiply drastically when considering outsourcing direct supply chain capabilities. The organizational design needs include moving work product to an external outsourcer, and they also include the need to establish new organizational capabilities to effectively manage the relationship.

Summary

The impact of vertical integration, horizontal integration, and outsourcing are significant business ecosystem events. Each impacts the business in different ways, and each requires a full review of organizational capabilities as one explores the organizational design implications. Being able to view the business as a system and apply all of the disciplines will help to drive planful and intentional changes. When done well, this will ensure that market opportunities are captured in the most effective and efficient manner possible.

Selecting a Consulting Firm

Organizational design that sticks, performed within the context of the business ecosystem, requires practice. Using a multi-disciplinary approach ensures a much higher success rate for initiatives. The real challenge for most companies is that they do not have dedicated organizational design practitioners who can stay active in their profession and keep their skills sharp. Only the largest of companies have this level of resource available. This challenge is made even more difficult by the extensive skill requirements in order to wield all 7 disciplines and bring them to bear on business needs. Organizational design, along with the other six disciplines need to be applied at the right level, right time, and sequenced/connected properly to drive the desired change and the greatest adoption.

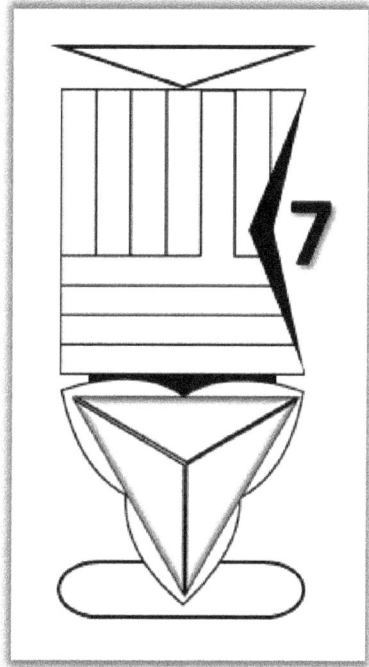

The importance of a **holistic systems view** cannot be understated. As illustrated in Figure 26, an organizational design need is most often accompanied by other needs. Rarely are business issues solved exclusively through *only* one of the seven disciplines. When selecting a consulting firm to perform any of the seven disciplines, you will be best-served to ensure that the firm has a professional vantage point rooted in systems thinking. Even when you have determined that you only indeed need one of the disciplines, and that you're managing the rest through other means, the consulting firm should be fully-mindful of their impact to the business ecosystem and other work streams. The ability to perform a contracted discipline such as organizational design is just as important as being able to collaborate both internally and with other external firms. After all, it is the performance of your entire business ecosystem that's on the line. Maximizing the benefits to the business requires full engagement and partnership.

At Alonos®, every one of our constituents is fully versed in systems thinking and the application of IRA-7 so that our clients gain maximum value and success from each engagement. This is true of our consultants and it is equally true of every other position in our firm. We believe that the systems thinking approach and the 7 disciplines are the only way to maximize results, so much so that every person in our firm is trained in them.

The firms you want to work with are those that are focused on **capability-building**. An external consulting firm should have your capabilities in mind with everything they do. At our firm, we believe in business-building! It is our mission to build capabilities in our client's businesses and people. We have had consistent success by building project teams using a combination of internal and external resources. External subject matter experts/practitioners are partnered with internal resources; this enables a rapid initiation, controls costs, and helps to ensure knowledge transfer.

Temporary engagements should be the rule when it comes to consulting. Consulting is different than outsourcing. There are many firms that are not really interested in being a consultant to you; instead, they are interested in being an outsourcer. Consultants come in, help you build capability, and leave you in a position where you can run and operate that capability on your own. If an external firm desires to perform a set of services for you on a regular, consistent, and day-to-day basis, they are an outsourcer.

Get a **good mix.** Our firm is intentional about the resources we partner with and employ. We select for practitioners who have a mix of experience across industries and practice areas. We supply people who have deep expertise in multiple disciplines along with the education and credentials to support on-going development of the disciplines' bodies of knowledge. We develop our people toward this goal: to be practitioners in all seven. Consequently, we are in a unique position to help you build organizational capabilities.

References

Ashkenas, R. (2013). *Change Management Needs to Change.* Harvard Business Review. (April 16).

Barnard, C. (1948). *The functions of the executive.* Cambridge, MA: Harvard University Press.

Blenko, M.W., Mankins, M.C., & Rogers, P. (2010). *Decide and deliver: 5 steps to breakthrough performance in your organization.* Boston, MA: Bain & Company.

Burton, R.M., Obel, B, & Hakonsson, D.D. (2015). *Organizational Design: A step-by-step approach.* (3rd Ed.) Cambridge, United Kingdom: Cambridge University Press.

Dale, E. (1967). *Organization.* American Management Association

DePass, D. (2016). *Select Comfort's second quarter beats earnings expectations but misses on sales: Bedmaker still feeling impact from ERP computer installation.* (July 20, 2016). Star Tribune. Retrieved November 2017 from: http://www.startribune.com/select-comfort-s-2q-beats-profit-expectations-but-misses-on-sales/387702561/

Drucker, P. (1993). *Concept of the corporation.* London, U.K.: Transaction Publishers.

Dun & Bradstreet. (2013). *D&B Global & U.S. Business Data.* (DB-3662 11/13). Retrieved November 2017 from: http://www.dnb.com/content/dam/english/dnb-data-insight/global-data-collection/dnb_global_and_us_business_data.pdf

Frick, W. (2015). Are successful CEOs just lucky? *Harvard Business Review* (November 16, 2015). Retrieved on November 21, 2017 from: https://hbr.org/2015/11/are-successful-ceos-just-lucky

Galbraith, J. (1995). *Designing Organizations: An executive briefing on strategy, structure, and process.* San Francisco, CA: Jossey-Bass Publishers.

Heidrick & Struggles (2015). *A board member's guide to CEO succession trends.* Heidrick & Struggles International, Inc.

Jackson, M.C. (2009). Fifty years of systems thinking for management. *The Journal of the Operational Research Society, 60*(1), 524-532.

Kanaracus, C. (2013). *Senate to probe failed Air Force ERP software project.* (January 25, 2013). Computerworld. Retrieved November 2017 from: https://www.computerworld.com/article/2494760/vertical-it/senate-to-probe-failed-air-force-erp-software-project.html

McCallum, D., & Henshaw, G.H. (1855) *Organizational diagram of the New York and Erie Railroad* [Public domain].

McCraw, T.K. (2009). *Prophet of Innovation: Joseph Schumpeter and Creative Destruction.* Fellows of Harvard College.

Mimic, V. (2016). *Why Projects Fail?* Project-Management.com. Retrieved October 2017, from: https://project-management.com/why-projects-fail/

Nadeau, M. & Dedijer, J. (2017). *Failwatching: The best product and brand failures of 2016* (Presentation).

Porter, M.E. (1998). *Competitive Advantage: Creating and sustaining superior performance.* New York, NY: The Free Press.

Rogers, B. (2016). *Why 84% of Companies Fail at Digital Transformation.* (January 7). Forbes. Retrieved October 2017, from: https://www.forbes.com/sites/brucerogers/2016/01/07/why-84-of-companies-fail-at-digital-transformation/#1d2b3a8e397b

Rosa, S. (2013). *Ron Johnson's Attempt to Fix JCPenney's Brand was Completely Backwards.* Business Insider (April). Retrieved November 2017 from: http://www.businessinsider.com/why-ron-johnson-failed-at-branding-jcp-2013-4

Schloetzer, J.D., Tonello, M., & Aguilar, M. (2015). *CEO Succession Practices: 2017 edition.* The Conference Board.

Senge, P.M. (2006). *The fifth discipline: The art & practice of the learning organization.* New York, NY: Doubleday.

Skarzauskiene, A. (2010). Managing complexity: systems thinking as a catalyst of the organizational performance. *Measuring Business Excellence, 14*(4), 49-64. doi: 10.1108/13683041011093758

Soltanzadeh, S., & Mooney, M. (2016). Systems thinking and team performance analysis. *International Sport Coaching Journal (3),* 184-191.

Tearcy, M. & Wiersema, F. (1995). *The Disciplines of Market Leaders.* New York, NY: Harper Collins Publishers, Inc.

Thibodeau, P. (2017). *MillerCoors seeks $100M in damages from IT contractor.* (March 21, 2017). Computerworld. Retrieved November 2017 from: https://www.computerworld.com/article/3183470/it-outsourcing/millercoors-seeks-100m-in-damages-from-it-contractor.html

Ulrich, D. (1987). Organizational capability as a competitive advantage: Human resource professionals as strategic partners. *Human Resource Planning, 10* (4), 169-184.

Ulrich, D. (1993). Profiling organizational competitiveness: Cultivating capabilities. *Human Resource Planning, 16* (3), 1-17.

Ulrich, D., & Smallwood, N. (2004). Capitalizing on capabilities. *Harvard Business Review, 82* (6), 119-127.

Whyte, A. (2016). *Gartner: 75% of all ERP Projects Fail – But Why?* The Office of Finance, London, United Kingdom.

www.ingramcontent.com/pod-product-compliance
Lightning Source LLC
Chambersburg PA
CBHW031404180326
41458CB00043B/6607/J